casual cooking

Meat feast

casual cooking

Meat feast

LOVE FOOD™

This edition published by Parragon Books Ltd in 2015
LOVE FOOD is an imprint of Parragon Books Ltd

Parragon Books Ltd
Chartist House
15–17 Trim Street
Bath BA1 1HA, UK
www.parragon.com/lovefood

ISBN 978-1-4723-8489-8

Printed in China

Cover photography by Charlie Richards
Designed by Beth Kalynka
Nutritional analysis by Judith Wills

Notes for the Reader
This book uses both metric and imperial measurements. Follow the same units of
measurement throughout; do not mix metric and imperial. All spoon measurements are
level: teaspoons are assumed to be 5 ml, and tablespoons are assumed to be 15 ml. Unless
otherwise stated, milk is assumed to be full fat, eggs and individual vegetables are medium,
and pepper is freshly ground black pepper. Unless otherwise stated, all root vegetables
should be peeled prior to using. For best results, use a food thermometer when cooking
meat – check the latest government guidelines for current advice.

Garnishes, decorations and serving suggestions are all optional and not necessarily included
in the recipe ingredients or method. Any optional ingredients and seasoning to taste are
not included in the nutritional analysis. The times given are an approximate guide only.
Preparation times differ according to the techniques used by different people and the
cooking times may also vary from those given. Optional ingredients, variations or serving
suggestions have not been included in the time calculations. Nutritional values are per
serving (Serves...) or per item (Makes...).

contents

mighty steak out

Grilled, griddled, pan-fried or cooked on a barbecue, steaks of all sorts are always popular but if served plain can be unexciting. Liven them up with exciting rubs and marinades and stop them feeling lonely by adding salads and sides. There are lots of meats to choose from, and you can even have 'meaty' fish.

raise the steaks

italian turkey steaks	8
rump steak sandwiches	10
tuna with chilli & ginger sauce	12
drunk chuck steak	14
blade steak in a green herb marinade	16
gammon steaks with parsley sauce	18
sichuan peppered steak	20
pork fillet with roasted rhubarb	22
grilled steak tortilla	24
BEEF STEAK	26
tarragon turkey steaks	28
halibut steaks with salsa verde	30
rib-eye steak	32
steak with rocket & parmesan	34
beef with gravy & mustard mash	36
boozy beef steaks	38
spice-crusted salmon steaks	40
new york strip steak with béarnaise sauce	42

italian turkey steaks

prep: 15 mins
cook: 50 mins–1 hour

1 tbsp olive oil

4 turkey escalopes or steaks

2 red peppers, deseeded and sliced

1 red onion, sliced

2 garlic cloves, finely chopped

300 ml/10 fl oz passata

150 ml/5 fl oz medium white wine

1 tbsp chopped fresh marjoram

400 g/14 oz canned cannellini beans,
  drained and rinsed

3 tbsp fresh white breadcrumbs

salt and pepper

fresh basil sprigs, to garnish

variation

Swap chicken breast fillets for the turkey and haricot beans for the cannellini beans.

1. Heat the oil in a flameproof casserole, add the turkey and cook over a medium heat for 5–10 minutes, turning occasionally, until browned all over. Transfer to a plate using a slotted spoon.

2. Add the red peppers and onion to the casserole and cook over a low heat, stirring occasionally, for 5 minutes, or until softened. Add the garlic and cook for a further 2 minutes.

3. Return the turkey to the casserole and add the passata, wine and marjoram. Season to taste with salt and pepper. Bring to the boil, then reduce the heat, cover and simmer, stirring occasionally, for 25–30 minutes, or until the turkey is cooked through and the juices run clear when a skewer is inserted into the thickest part of the meat. Meanwhile, preheat the grill to medium.

4. Stir the cannellini beans into the casserole and simmer for a further 5 minutes. Sprinkle the breadcrumbs over the top and place under the preheated grill for 2–3 minutes, or until golden. Serve immediately, garnished with basil sprigs.

serves 4

cals: 384   fat: 6.8g   sat fat: 1.5g   fibre: 6.5g   carbs: 23.2g   sugar: 9.8g   salt: 1.4g   protein: 48g

rump steak sandwiches

prep: 20-25 mins
cook: 20-25 mins

8 slices thick white bread

butter, softened, for spreading

2 handfuls mixed salad leaves

3 tbsp olive oil

2 onions, thinly sliced

675 g/1 lb 8 oz rump steak,
   2.5 cm/1 inch thick

1 tbsp Worcestershire sauce

2 tbsp wholegrain mustard

2 tbsp water

salt and pepper

variation

Try other types of fresh bread, like wholemeal, granary or multigrain, to make these delicious sandwiches.

1. Spread each slice of bread with some butter and add a few salad leaves to the four bottom slices.

2. Heat 2 tablespoons of the oil in a large frying pan over a medium heat. Add the onions and cook, stirring occasionally, for 10–15 minutes, or until softened and golden brown. Using a slotted spoon, transfer to a plate and set aside.

3. Increase the heat to high and add the remaining oil to the pan. Add the steak, season to taste with pepper and seal on both sides. Reduce the heat to medium and cook for 2½–3 minutes on each side for rare, or until cooked to your liking. Transfer the steak to the plate with the onions.

4. Add the Worcestershire sauce, mustard and water to the pan. Use a wooden spoon to scrape the sediment from the base of the pan. When the liquid has deglazed the pan, add the onions and stir. Season to taste with salt and pepper.

5. Thinly slice the steak across the grain, divide between the four bottom slices of bread and cover with the onion and mustard dressing. Cover with the top slices of bread and press down gently. Serve immediately.

cals: 697   fat: 35.7g   sat fat: 14.6g   fibre: 5.4g   carbs: 47.2   sugar: 5.5g   salt: 2.3g   protein: 44.4g

tuna with chilli & ginger sauce

prep: 20 mins
cook: 20 mins

4 tuna steaks, 2 cm/¾ inch thick,
about 175 g/6 oz each

2 tbsp olive oil, plus extra for oiling

salt and pepper

lime wedges, to serve

chilli & ginger marinade

100 g/3½ oz soft brown sugar

125 ml/4 fl oz water

2.5-cm/1-inch piece fresh ginger,
thinly shredded

1 bird's eye chilli or jalapeño chilli,
deseeded and finely chopped

1 large garlic clove, crushed

juice of ½ lime

top tip

Bird's eye chillies are small and fiery-hot
Jalapeños have a more moderate level of
heat The natural oils in chillies can
cause irritation, so wear disposable
gloves when preparing them.

1. This recipe requires a barbecue. To make
the marinade, put the sugar and water in a
small saucepan and bring to the boil. Boil for
7–8 minutes, until syrupy. Add the ginger,
chilli, garlic and lime juice, and boil for
another minute. Pour into a bowl
and leave to cool completely.

2. Put the tuna steaks in a single layer in a
shallow dish. Brush on both sides with the
oil and rub with salt and pepper to taste.

Pour the cold marinade over the tuna steaks,
turning to coat. Cover with clingfilm and leave
to marinate in the refrigerator for 30–60
minutes, turning occasionally.

3. Preheat the barbecue to hot. Oil the grill
rack and a hinged wire grill basket. Place
the tuna steaks in the basket, reserving the
marinade. Cook over hot coals for 2 minutes.
Turn and cook the other side for 1 minute.
Remove from the basket and wrap in foil to
keep warm.

4. Pour the reserved marinade into a small
saucepan. Bring to the boil and boil for
2 minutes. Pour into a small jug. Arrange the
tuna on serving plates and serve immediately
with lime wedges and the hot marinade.

cals: 375   fat: 9.3g   sat fat: 1.4g   fibre: 0.3g   carbs: 28.4g   sugar: 25.1g   salt: 0.9g   protein: 43.1g

drunk chuck steak

prep: 10-15 mins, plus marinating & standing
cook: 15-25 mins

4 chuck steaks, 350 g/12 oz each

marinade
4 tbsp olive oil
100 ml/3½ fl oz good quality red wine
1 small bunch fresh thyme,
    leaves picked
1 small bunch fresh rosemary,
    leaves picked
2 garlic cloves, crushed
1 tbsp Dijon mustard
1 tsp salt
1 tsp pepper

top tip

Enjoy these sumptuous steaks with simple sides, such as oven-baked potato wedges or chips and a mixed leaf salad.

1. Place all of the marinade ingredients in a shallow non-metallic dish, large enough to hold all of the steaks in a single layer. Mix the ingredients together.

2. Add the steaks to the marinade, turning a few times to coat. Cover and chill in the refrigerator for a minimum of 4 hours, or for up to 12 hours if time allows. Turn once, mid-way through marinating.

3. Remove from the refrigerator 1 hour before cooking, to allow the meat to return to room temperature. Discard the marinade.

4. Preheat a griddle pan over a high heat and cook the steaks for 5 minutes on each side for medium-rare, or until cooked to your liking. Cook the steaks in batches if necessary. Set aside to rest for 5 minutes before serving.

serves 4

cals: 818   fat: 60.7g   sat fat: 24.8g   fibre: 0.1g   carbs: 0.9g   sugar: 0.2g   salt: 1.3g   protein: 66.2g

blade steak in a green herb marinade

prep: 15 mins, plus marinating and standing
cook: 12-22 mins, plus resting

4 top blade steaks, 350 g/12 oz each

marinade
4 tbsp olive oil
1 tbsp light muscovado sugar
2 tbsp red wine vinegar
2 tbsp chopped fresh flat-leaf parsley
2 tbsp chopped fresh basil
2 tbsp chopped fresh tarragon
2 tbsp chopped fresh thyme
2 garlic cloves, crushed
1 tsp salt
1 tsp pepper

1. Place all of the marinade ingredients in a shallow non-metallic dish, large enough to hold all of the steaks in a single layer. Mix the ingredients together.

2. Add the steaks to the marinade, turning a few times to coat. Cover and chill in the refrigerator for a minimum of 4 hours, or for up to 12 hours if time allows. Turn once, mid-way through marinating.

3. Remove from the refrigerator 1 hour before cooking, to allow the meat to return to room temperature. Discard the marinade.

4. Preheat a griddle pan over a high heat and cook the steaks for 5 minutes on each side for medium-rare, or until cooked to your liking. Cook the steaks in batches if necessary. Set aside to rest for 5 minutes before serving.

serves 4

cals: 868   fat: 67.9g   sat fat: 27.3g   fibre: trace   carbs: 1.5g   sugar: 1.5g   salt: 1.3g   protein: 60g

gammon steaks with
parsley sauce

4 unsmoked gammon steaks, 2 cm/
   ¾ inch thick, about 200 g/7 oz each
vegetable oil, for brushing

parsley sauce
25 g/1 oz unsalted butter
1 shallot, finely chopped
3 tbsp plain flour
175 ml/6 fl oz ham or chicken stock
250 ml/9 fl oz milk
5 tbsp chopped fresh parsley
squeeze of lemon juice
½ tsp mustard powder
salt and white pepper

top tip

Serve with boiled new potatoes (tossed in chopped parsley) and seasonal veg like broad beans or peas and carrots.

1. First make the parsley sauce. Melt the butter in a frying pan over a medium-low heat. Add the shallot and cook for 2–3 minutes, until soft but not coloured.

2. Remove the frying pan from the heat and stir in the flour. Return to the heat and cook for 1 minute, stirring. Reduce the heat to low, and whisk in the stock and milk. Keep whisking until the sauce starts to bubble. Stir in the parsley, then add the lemon juice, mustard, pepper and a pinch of salt. Simmer gently, stirring often, for 20 minutes.

3. Meanwhile, remove the rind but not the fat from the gammon steaks. Slash the fat at 2-cm/¾-inch intervals. Brush the steaks with oil on both sides.

4. Heat a ridged griddle pan over a high heat. Cook the steaks on one side for 5–6 minutes. Once they start to colour on the underside, cover with a lid and reduce the heat to medium. Turn and cook the other side for 5 minutes, covered. Cook the steaks in batches if necessary.

5. Place the steaks on warmed serving plates, pour the sauce over them and serve.

serves 4

cals: 463   fat: 22.4g   sat fat: 8.9g   fibre: 0.9g   carbs: 14.4g   sugar: 4.1g   salt: 6.7g   protein: 49.5g

sichuan peppered steak

prep: 30 mins, plus marinating
cook: 6-8 mins, plus resting

4 flank steaks or thin rump steaks, about 175 g/6 oz each
½ head Chinese leaves, thinly sliced
25 g/1 oz fresh mint leaves
25 g/1 oz fresh coriander leaves
½ red onion, thinly sliced
squeeze of lime juice
oil, for brushing
salt and pepper
lime wedges, to garnish

marinade
1 whole garlic bulb, cloves separated and peeled
¼ tsp salt
2 tbsp Sichuan peppercorns
1 tbsp black peppercorns
2 tsp soft brown sugar
1 bird's eye chilli, deseeded and finely chopped
4 tbsp soy sauce
juice of 1 lime

1. This recipe requires a barbecue. Place the steaks between two sheets of clingfilm and pound with a meat mallet until flattened to 5 mm/¼ inch. Slice each steak in half and place in a single layer in a shallow dish.

2. To make the marinade, place the garlic and salt in a mortar and pound with a pestle. Add both types of peppercorn, the sugar and chilli, and pound to a paste. Stir in the soy sauce and lime juice. Pour over the meat, turning to coat. Cover with clingfilm and leave to marinate at room temperature for 1 hour, or preferably overnight in the refrigerator.

3. Preheat the barbecue to medium-hot. Arrange the Chinese leaves, mint and coriander leaves in a shallow serving dish. Scatter with the onion slices and sprinkle with salt, pepper and lime juice to taste.

4. Remove the meat from the marinade, scraping off any solids and discarding the marinade. Pat dry with kitchen paper and lightly brush with oil. Thread concertina-style onto four metal or pre-soaked wooden skewers. Oil the grill rack.

5. Cook the meat over medium-hot coals for 3–4 minutes on each side, until browned. Transfer to a dish, remove the skewers and leave to rest for 5 minutes. Arrange on top of the salad and sprinkle with any juices from the meat. Serve immediately, garnished with the lime wedges.

serves 4

cals: 273   fat: 10.9g   sat fat: 3.1g   fibre: 1g   carbs: 3.8g   sugar: 1.7g   salt: 1.7g   protein: 38.3g

pork fillet with roasted rhubarb

prep: 25 mins
cook: 55-60 mins, plus resting

800 g/1 lb 12 oz boneless pork fillet

olive oil

1 tsp sea salt flakes

½ tsp black pepper

10 small sprigs of fresh rosemary

125 ml/4 fl oz chicken stock

175 g/6 oz pink rhubarb stalks, trimmed and sliced diagonally into 4-cm/1½-inch lengths

1 tbsp honey

1. Preheat the oven to 190°C/375°F/Gas Mark 5. Using the tip of a sharp knife, score the fat, but not the flesh, of the pork at 1-cm/½-inch intervals. Tie the meat with kitchen string to form a neat roll. You can ask your butcher to do both of these.

2. Place the meat in a small roasting tin. Rub with oil and then with the sea salt and black pepper, rubbing them in well. Insert the rosemary sprigs into the slits in the fat. Roast in the preheated oven for 40 minutes.

3. Pour in the stock. Arrange the rhubarb around the meat and drizzle with the honey. Roast for another 10–15 minutes, until the rhubarb is tender and starting to colour at the edges.

4. Transfer the pork and rhubarb to a warmed serving platter, reserving the pan juices. Make a tent over the meat with foil and leave to rest for 10 minutes in a warm place.

5. Place the roasting tin on the hob over a medium-high heat. Let bubble rapidly to reduce the pan juices, adding any that have flowed from the meat, for 3–4 minutes, until slightly thickened. Check the seasoning, strain into a jug and serve with the meat.

serves 4

cals: 477   fat: 23g   sat fat: 8g   fibre: 0.8g   carbs: 6.7g   sugar: 4.8g   salt: 2g   protein: 60.9g

grilled steak tortilla

675 g/1 lb 8 oz sirloin steak

warmed corn tortillas and shredded lettuce, to serve

marinade

2 tbsp olive oil

2 garlic cloves, crushed

juice of 1 lime

1 tbsp ground cumin

1 tbsp mild chilli powder

1 tsp salt

½ tsp pepper

½ tsp ground cinnamon

¼–½ tsp cayenne pepper

pineapple salsa

400 g/14 oz diced fresh pineapple

2 bird's eye or jalapeño chillies (or use 1 red and 1 green chilli), deseeded and finely chopped

1 small red onion, finely diced

½ teaspoon salt

juice of 1 lime

1. To make the marinade, combine the oil, garlic, lime juice, cumin, chilli powder, salt, pepper, cinnamon and cayenne pepper in a bowl. Spread over the steak, coating both sides. Cover and refrigerate for at least 30 minutes or up to 24 hours.

2. Preheat the barbecue to high. To make the salsa, put the pineapple, chillies, onion, salt and lime juice into a medium-sized bowl and stir to mix.

3. Place the steak on the barbecue rack over a high heat and cook to taste, about 5 minutes each side for medium. Remove from the heat, cover loosely with foil and leave to rest for 5 minutes. Thinly slice and serve with warmed tortillas, shredded lettuce and the pineapple salsa.

top tip

Everyone can assemble their own tortillas, so this dish creates a fantastic flavourful family supper for sharing.

serves 4

cals: 410   fat: 15.3g   sat fat: 3.6g   fibre: 4.3g   carbs: 30.4g   sugar: 11.8g   salt: 2.5g   protein: 39g

beef steak

blue

Prepare the steak as instructed, then place in the preheated pan and seal both sides of the meat. The steak should be browned on the outside, but still raw in the middle. When pressed it should bulge slightly, and the indentation should remain in the meat.

rare

Prepare the steak as instructed, then place in the preheated pan and seal both sides of the meat. The steak should be warm through the middle, browned on the outside, but still pink in the centre. It will be slightly more resistant to the touch than a blue steak.

Medium rare

Prepare the steak as instructed, then place in the preheated pan and seal both sides of the meat. The steak should be browned on the outside, but still slightly pink in the centre. When pressed, the indentation should remain, but will quickly pool with cooking juices.

medium

Prepare the steak as instructed, then place in the preheated pan and seal both sides of the meat. The steak should be more brown than pink, but still slightly pink in the centre. When pressed, a medium steak will offer some resistance and the indentation will spring back into place.

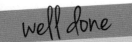

well done

Prepare the steak as instructed, then place in the preheated pan and seal both sides of the meat. The steak should be brown all the way through. When pressed, the steak will offer a good deal of resistance and will spring immediately back into place.

tarragon turkey steaks

prep: 15 mins
cook: 10–16 mins

4 turkey steaks, about 175 g/6 oz each

4 tsp wholegrain mustard

8 fresh tarragon sprigs, plus extra
 to garnish

4 smoked back bacon rashers

salt and pepper

salad leaves, to serve (optional)

top tip

Tarragon has a distinctive aniseed-type flavour that goes well with turkey and chicken, as well as fish and eggs. French tarragon is superior in flavour to Russian (wild) tarragon, which is milder.

1. This recipe requires a barbecue. Preheat the barbecue. Season the turkey to taste with salt and pepper, and, using a round-bladed knife, spread the mustard evenly over the turkey.

2. Place 2 tarragon sprigs on top of each turkey breast and wrap a bacon rasher around it to hold the tarragon in place. Secure with a cocktail stick.

3. Cook the turkey over medium-hot coals for 5–8 minutes on each side, or until cooked through. Transfer to serving plates and garnish with tarragon sprigs. Serve immediately with salad leaves.

cals: 261   fat: 6.6g   sat fat: 2.3g   fibre: 0.3g   carbs: 0.6g   sugar: 0.1g   salt: 1.9g   protein: 47g

halibut steaks with salsa verde

2–3 tbsp olive oil, plus extra for oiling
juice of ½ lemon
¼ tsp sea salt
¼ tsp pepper
4 halibut steaks, 2 cm/¾ inch thick,
    about 175–225 g/6–8 oz each
lemon wedges, to serve

salsa verde
2 anchovy fillets, rinsed and drained
50 g/1¾ oz stale breadcrumbs
25 g/1 oz fresh flat-leaf parsley leaves
25 g/1 oz fresh basil leaves
2 tbsp capers, rinsed
1 garlic clove, crushed
2 tbsp lemon juice
125 ml/4 fl oz olive oil
salt and pepper

top tip

Salsa verde is ideal for jazzing up roasted veg, grilled meats, cold meats, fish and seafood.

1. This recipe requires a barbecue. To make the marinade, combine the oil, lemon juice, sea salt and pepper in a shallow, non-metallic dish. Add the halibut steaks and turn to coat. Cover with clingfilm and leave to marinate in the refrigerator for 1 hour, turning halfway through.

2. Preheat the barbecue. Combine all the salsa ingredients in a food processor and briefly pulse 4–5 times to a rough paste. Pour into a bowl and set aside.

3. Oil the grill rack and a hinged wire grill basket. Place the halibut in the basket, reserving the marinade. Cook over hot coals, brushing with the reserved marinade, for 4–6 minutes on each side, or until golden and cooked through.

4. Carefully remove the halibut from the basket and place on serving plates. Serve immediately with the salsa verde and lemon wedges for squeezing over.

serves 4

cals: 594   fat: 44.7g   sat fat: 6.4g   fibre: 0.9g   carbs: 8.5g   sugar: 0.9g   salt: 2.5g   protein: 39.1g

rib-eye steak in a boozy bourbon marinade

prep: 15 mins, plus marinating and standing
cook: 22 mins, plus resting

4 rib-eye steaks, 350 g/12 oz each

2 tbsp olive oil

2 tbsp butter

marinade

2 tbsp extra virgin olive oil

200 ml/7 fl oz good quality bourbon

1 small bunch fresh thyme, leaves
    picked

1 tsp dried oregano

2 garlic cloves, crushed

1 tsp salt

1 tsp pepper

1. Place all of the marinade ingredients in a shallow non-metallic dish, large enough to hold all of the steaks in a single layer. Mix the ingredients together.

2. Add the steaks to the marinade, turning a few times to coat. Cover and chill in the refrigerator for a minimum of 4 hours, or for up to 12 hours if time allows. Turn once, mid-way through marinating.

3. Remove from the refrigerator at least 1 hour before cooking, to allow the meat to return to room temperature.

4. Preheat a large frying pan over a high heat and add the oil and butter. Add the steaks to the pan, reserving the marinade. Cook them for 5 minutes on each side for medium-rare, or until cooked to your liking. Cook the steaks in batches if necessary. Set aside to rest for 5 minutes before serving.

5. Meanwhile, reduce the heat to medium-high, pour the reserved marinade into the pan, and flambé to create a sauce. Serve the steaks with the sauce poured over the top.

serves 4

cals: 1101   fat: 70g   sat fat: 30g   fibre: 0.4g   carbs: 1.3g   sugar: trace   salt: 2.3g   protein: 87.1g

steak with rocket & parmesan

prep: 15 mins, plus standing
cook: 7–10 mins, plus resting

4 sirloin steaks, 3 cm/1¼ inches thick, about 225 g/8 oz each

olive oil, for oiling

100 g/3½ oz rocket

salt and pepper

grated Parmesan cheese and balsamic vinegar, to serve

top tip

Rocket leaves, with their dark green serrated leaves, have a distinctive peppery flavour, so watercress is an ideal substitute.

1. This recipe requires a barbecue. Preheat the barbecue to high. Snip the fat on the steaks at 1-cm/½-inch intervals to stop it curling and shrinking as it cooks. Sprinkle both sides with salt and pepper. Cover and leave to stand at room temperature for 30 minutes.

2. Heap some of the coals on one side of the barbecue leaving a slightly cooler area with a single layer of coals. Oil the barbecue rack.

3. Cook the steaks on the hottest part of the grill for 2–3 minutes on each side until brown. Move to the cooler part of the barbecue and cook to your liking: rare 2½ minutes, medium-rare 3–3½ minutes and medium 4 minutes. Transfer to a board and leave to rest for 5 minutes.

4. Carve each steak into 2-cm/¾-inch thick slices and transfer to individual serving plates. Divide the rocket among the plates. Sprinkle over the Parmesan, drizzle with balsamic vinegar and serve immediately.

serves 4

cals: 419   fat: 18.3g   sat fat: 7.8g   fibre: 0.5g   carbs: 2.5g   sugar: 1.3g   salt: 2.1g   protein: 57.6g

beef with gravy & mustard mash

prep: 20 mins
cook: 1 hour 20 mins

2 tsp vegetable oil

225 g/8 oz extra-lean stewing steak,
  cut into 8 pieces

10 small shallots, peeled but left whole

1 garlic clove, crushed

1 tomato, chopped

100 g/3½ oz mushrooms, finely sliced

150 ml/5 fl oz red wine

100 ml/3½ fl oz chicken stock

bouquet garni

1 tsp cornflour

salt and pepper

mustard mash

2 floury potatoes, sliced

1½ –2 tbsp skimmed milk, heated

1 tsp Dijon mustard, or to taste

1. Preheat the oven to 180°C/350°F/Gas Mark 4.

2. Heat the oil in a flameproof casserole. Add the meat and shallots and cook over a high heat, stirring, for 4–5 minutes, or until the meat is browned on all sides. Add the garlic, tomato, mushrooms, wine, stock and bouquet garni. Bring to a simmer, cover and transfer to the preheated oven to cook for 45–60 minutes, or until everything is tender.

3. Meanwhile, to make the mustard mash, place the potatoes in a saucepan of boiling water and simmer for 20 minutes, or until just tender. Remove from the heat, drain well and return to the saucepan. Add the milk and mash well. Stir in the mustard and keep warm.

4. Use a slotted spoon to remove the meat and vegetables from the casserole and transfer to a warmed serving dish. Cook the gravy on the hob over a high heat until reduced by half. Reduce the heat, remove the bouquet garni and adjust the seasoning, adding salt and pepper if needed.

5. Mix the cornflour to a paste with a little cold water. Add to the gravy, stirring well, and bring back to a simmer. Pour the gravy over the meat and vegetables and serve with the mustard mash.

cals: 499   fat: 9.3g   sat fat: 2.4g   fibre: 7g   carbs: 60.8g   sugar: 13.6g   salt: 3.7g   protein: 32.8g

boozy beef steaks

prep: 15 mins, plus marinating
cook: 13–26 mins

4 beef steaks, about 225 g/8 oz each

4 tbsp whisky or brandy

2 tbsp soy sauce

1 tbsp dark muscovado sugar

tomato slices

pepper

fresh flat-leaf parsley sprigs,
   to garnish

garlic bread, to serve (optional)

top tip

Depending on your budget, rump or sirloin steaks are both good choices for this recipe.

1. This recipe requires a barbecue. Snip the fat on the steaks at 1-cm/½-inch intervals to stop it curling and shrinking as it cooks. Place the meat in a shallow, non-metallic dish.

2. Mix the whisky, soy sauce, sugar and pepper to taste together in a small bowl, stirring until the sugar dissolves. Pour the mixture over the steak. Cover with clingfilm and leave to marinate in the refrigerator for at least 2 hours.

3. Preheat the barbecue. Cook the meat over hot coals, searing the meat over the hottest part of the barbecue for 2 minutes on each side.

4. Move the meat to an area with slightly less intense heat and cook for a further 4–10 minutes on each side, depending on how well done you like your steaks.

5. Lightly barbecue the tomato slices for 1–2 minutes. Transfer the meat and the tomatoes to serving plates. Garnish with parsley sprigs and serve immediately with garlic bread.

serves 4

cals: 258   fat: 7.4g   sat fat: 2.6g   fibre: 0.4g   carbs: 3.3g   sugar: 2.6g   salt: 0.8g   protein: 37.7g

spice-crusted salmon steaks

prep: 20 mins
cook: 8 mins

1 tbsp cumin seeds

1 tsp coriander seeds

4 salmon steaks, about 175 g/6 oz each, skin on

olive oil, for brushing

salt and pepper

coriander & spring onion pesto

2 small garlic cloves

large bunch fresh coriander, large stems discarded

large bunch fresh flat-leaf parsley, large stems discarded

3 spring onions, white and light green parts only

1–2 bird's eye chillies or jalapeño chillies, deseeded

125 ml/4 fl oz olive oil

juice of 1 lemon

1 tsp salt

1. This recipe requires a barbecue. To make the pesto, chop the garlic in a food processor. Add the coriander, parsley, spring onions and chillies and process until finely chopped. Add the oil, lemon juice and salt and process until well combined. Set aside.

2. Preheat the barbecue to high. Coarsely grind the cumin seeds and coriander seeds in an electric spice grinder or in a mortar with a pestle. Brush the fish on both sides with oil, season with salt and pepper and coat lightly with the seed mixture.

3. Place the salmon on the barbecue rack skin-side down and cook over a high heat with the lid on for about 4 minutes. Turn the salmon over and cook on the other side for a further 4 minutes, until just cooked through. Serve immediately, topped with the pesto.

top tip

To boost your 5-a-day, serve these sizzling steaks with seasonal fresh veg such as broccoli and green beans.

new york strip steak with béarnaise sauce

prep: 20 mins, plus standing
cook: 25-35 mins, plus resting

4 porterhouse steaks, or entrecôte,
    225 g/8 oz each
1 tbsp olive oil or clarified butter
salt and pepper
sautéed potatoes or chips, to serve

    (optional)

béarnaise sauce
large bunch fresh tarragon
1 shallot, finely chopped
100 ml/3½ fl oz white wine vinegar
4 peppercorns
2 egg yolks
200 g/7 oz butter, cut into
small cubes

1. Remove the steaks from the refrigerator
20 minutes before cooking.

2. To make the béarnaise sauce, remove
the most tender leaves of the tarragon,
finely chop and set aside. Roughly chop
the tougher parts and add them to a small
saucepan with the shallot, vinegar and
peppercorns and simmer until it has reduced
to about 1 tablespoonful. Strain through a
sieve into a clean heatproof bowl.

3. Bring a small saucepan of water to the boil,
place the bowl on top, and gently whisk in the
egg yolks until the mixture thickens a little.
Add the butter a piece at a time and whisk it
in until the sauce is thick. Add the chopped
tarragon leaves and mix in. Taste and add salt
if needed. Turn off the heat and cover to keep
warm while you cook the steaks.

4. Season the steaks with salt and pepper
and brush with the oil. Heat a grill pan to
high and add the steaks. Cook quickly for
3–4 minutes on each side, check that they
are nicely seared, then cover and leave to
rest for 2 minutes before serving.

5. Stir the sauce in case it has separated, then
serve the steaks on lightly warmed plates with
sautéed potatoes and the béarnaise sauce
spooned over the top.

serves 4

cals: 719   fat: 55.8g   sat fat: 30.3g   fibre: 0.4g   carbs: 3.1g   sugar: 0.8g   salt: 1.9g   protein: 50.5g

Roasts are much easier to cook than many people think and are ideal for family gatherings and entertaining guests. They look great, smell amazing, taste wonderful and the choice of different meats, cuts and methods of preparation is huge.
Phew, it's roasting in here.

home to roast

roast chicken

prep: 20–25 mins
cook: 2 hours 5 mins, plus resting

1 chicken, weighing 2.25 kg/5 lb

55 g/2 oz soft butter

2 tbsp chopped fresh lemon thyme, plus extra sprigs to garnish

1 lemon, quartered

125 ml/4 fl oz white wine, plus extra if needed

salt and pepper

top tip

If your budget allows, choose a free-range or organic bird, as it will have been reared to higher welfare standards and usually has a superior flavour.

1. Preheat the oven to 220°C/425°F/Gas Mark 7. Place the chicken in a roasting tin.

2. Place the butter in a bowl, mix in the chopped thyme and season well with salt and pepper. Butter the chicken all over with the herb butter, inside and out, and place the lemon quarters inside the cavity. Pour the wine over the chicken.

3. Roast the chicken in the centre of the preheated oven for 15 minutes. Reduce the temperature to 190°C/375°F/Gas Mark 5 and continue to roast, basting frequently, for a further 1¾ hours. Cover with foil if the skin begins to brown too much. If the tin dries out, add a little more wine or water.

4. Test that the chicken is cooked by inserting a skewer into the thickest part of the meat and making sure the juices run clear. Remove from the oven.

5. Remove the chicken from the roasting tin and place on a warmed serving plate. Cover with foil and leave to rest for 10 minutes before carving.

6. Place the roasting tin on the hob and simmer the pan juices gently over a low heat until they have reduced and are thick and glossy. Season to taste with salt and pepper. Serve the chicken with the pan juices and garnish with thyme sprigs.

serves 6

cals: 612   fat: 46.1g   sat fat: 15.7g   fibre: 0.1g   carbs: 1.4g   sugar: 0.9g   salt: 1.1g   protein: 42g

roast pork belly with apple & mustard ketchup

prep: 30 mins, plus cooling
cook: 2 hours 10 mins, plus resting

small bunch fresh thyme

1 bulb of fennel bulb, sliced

1 onion, sliced

1.5 kg/3 lb 5 oz pork belly

575 ml/18 fl oz dry cider

300 ml/10 fl oz chicken stock

150 ml/5 fl oz cider vinegar

55 g/2 oz honey

1 tsp salt

1 tsp pepper

apple & mustard ketchup

juice of 2 lemons

55 g/2 oz sugar

3 cooking apples, peeled, cored and chopped

2 tbsp American-style yellow mustard

1. Preheat the oven to 190°C/375°F/Gas Mark 5.

2. Place the thyme, fennel and onion in a deep baking tray slightly bigger than the pork. Place the pork belly on top.

3. In a medium bowl, mix together the cider, stock, vinegar and honey.

4. Pour the cider mixture over the pork and then sprinkle over salt and pepper.

5. Place the baking tray in the oven. Cook for two hours, or until the pork meat is soft to the touch and crackling has formed. Check that the centre of the meat is no longer pink and the juices run clear.

6. Meanwhile, place all of the ketchup ingredients in a medium microwave-proof bowl. Cover with microwavable clingfilm and cook on high for 4 minutes, or until the apples start to fall apart. Blend the ketchup with a hand blender until smooth and leave to cool down.

7. Remove the pork from the oven and leave in a warm place to rest for 30 minutes. Strain the juices from the baking tray into a medium saucepan and simmer until the liquid is reduced by half.

8. Serve the pork with the cooking juices poured over the top and the ketchup on the side

top tip

For the ultimate sandwich,
just add bread and coleslaw.

cals: 1382   fat: 99.6g   sat fat: 54.3g   fibre: 5.3g   carbs: 52.7g   sugar: 42g   salt: 4.7   protein: 61.4g

roast turkey with cider sauce

prep: 25–30 mins, plus cooling
cook: 1¾ hours

1 boneless turkey breast roast,
   weighing 1 kg/2 lb 4 oz

1 tbsp sunflower or corn oil

salt and pepper

stuffing

25 g/1 oz butter

2 shallots, finely chopped

1 celery stick, finely chopped

1 cooking apple, peeled, cored and
   diced

115 g/4 oz prunes, stoned and
   chopped

55 g/2 oz raisins

3 tbsp chicken stock

4 tbsp dry cider

1 tbsp chopped fresh parsley

cider sauce

1 shallot, very finely chopped

300 ml/10 fl oz dry cider

125 ml/4 fl oz chicken stock

1 tsp cider vinegar

1. Preheat the oven to 190°C/375°F/Gas Mark 5.

2. To make the stuffing, melt the butter in a pan. Add the shallots and cook for 5 minutes. Add the celery and apple and cook for 5 minutes. Add the remaining stuffing ingredients, cover, and simmer gently for 5 minutes, or until all the liquid has been absorbed. Transfer to a bowl and leave to cool.

3. Place the turkey roast on a chopping board and slice almost completely through, from the thin side toward the thicker side. Open out, place between two sheets of clingfilm, and flatten with a meat mallet to an even thickness. Season to taste with salt. Spoon on the cooled stuffing, roll the roast around it, and tie with kitchen string.

4. Heat the oil in a roasting tin over medium heat, add the roast, and brown all over. Transfer to the oven and roast for 1 hour 10 minutes, or until cooked through and the juices run clear when the meat is pierced with a skewer. Remove the roast from the tin and cover with foil.

5. To make the sauce, pour off any fat from the tin and set over medium heat. Add the shallot and half the cider and cook for 1–2 minutes, scraping any sediment from the bottom of the pan. Add the remaining cider, stock and vinegar and cook for 10 minutes, or until reduced and thickened. Remove and discard the string from the turkey and cut into slices. Serve with the cider sauce.

top tip

This roast is perfect for a weekend gathering with family and friends, served with roasties and seasonal fresh veg.

serves 8

cals: 327   fat: 13.2   sat fat: 2.6g   fibre: 3.8g   carbs: 20.7g   sugar: 13.3g   salt: 0.8g   protein: 28.4g

whole tandoori chicken

prep: 25 mins, plus marinating
cook: 55 mins, plus resting

1 chicken, weighing 1.5 kg/3 lb 5 oz

2 tsp garam masala spice mix

300 ml/10 fl oz natural yogurt

1 onion, finely chopped

2 garlic cloves, crushed

2.5-cm/1-inch piece fresh ginger, peeled and grated

juice of 1 lemon

2 tbsp tomato purée

1 tsp chilli powder

1 tsp ground cumin

1 tsp turmeric

1 tbsp paprika (not smoked)

1 tsp salt

basmati rice

naan bread

lime wedges

hot lime pickle

top tip

Wash your hands thoroughly before and after handling raw chicken and be sure to clean utensils and work surfaces well with hot, soapy water.

1. Cut two slits into each chicken leg and two into each thigh. They should just reach the bone. Make two shallower cuts into the fleshiest part of each breast. These are to allow the marinade to penetrate into the meat.

2. Mix all of the remaining ingredients in a food processor and blend to a smooth paste. Place the chicken in a large, non-metallic dish and cover it in the paste, massaging it deep into the skin and flesh. Place the chicken, uncovered, in the refrigerator to marinate for as long as possible – preferably 24 hours.

3. Remove the chicken from the refrigerator an hour before cooking to warm it to room temperature. Preheat the oven to 220°C/425°F/Gas Mark 7. Place the chicken in the oven and cook, uncovered, for 20 minutes, then reduce the heat to 180°C/350°F/Gas Mark 4. Baste the chicken and cook for another 35 minutes. When fully cooked the juices will run clear. Turn off the oven and open the door, leaving the chicken inside to rest for 20 minutes.

cals: 613   fat: 40.2g   sat fat: 11.8g   fibre: 2.8g   carbs: 14.7g   sugar: 8.6g   salt: 2.6g   protein: 47g

plaice roasted with lime

4 plaice fillets, each about 250 g/9 oz

juice of 1 lime

3 tbsp extra virgin olive oil

1 large onion, finely chopped

3 garlic cloves, finely chopped

2–3 pickled jalapeño chillies
  (jalapeños en escabeche), chopped

6–8 tbsp chopped fresh coriander,
  plus extra sprigs to garnish

salt and pepper

lime wedges, to serve

variation

The distinctive tart flavour of lime juice works well with the other ingredients to flavour the plaice perfectly. Serve with lightly cooked vegetables like mangetout and baby carrots.

1. Preheat the oven to 180°C/350°F/Gas Mark 4.

2. Rinse the fish under cold running water and pat dry with kitchen paper. Place the fish fillets in a non-metallic bowl and season to taste with salt and pepper. Sprinkle the lime juice over the fish.

3. Heat the oil in a frying pan. Add the onion and garlic and cook, stirring frequently, for 2 minutes, or until softened. Remove the frying pan from the heat.

4. Place a third of the onion mixture and a little of the chillies and chopped coriander in the base of a shallow ovenproof dish or roasting tin. Arrange the fish on top. Top with the remaining onion mixture, chillies and chopped coriander.

5. Roast in the preheated oven for 15–20 minutes, or until the fish has become slightly opaque and firm to the touch. Garnish with coriander sprigs and serve immediately with lime wedges for squeezing over.

serves 4

cals: 351   fat: 15.9g   sat fat: 3.4g   fibre: 1.5g   carbs: 8g   sugar: 2.7g   salt: 1.7g   protein: 45.5g

roast duck with redcurrant sauce

4 duck breasts, skin on, about
    185 g/6½ oz each
4 shallots, finely chopped
salt and pepper

redcurrant sauce

2 garlic cloves, crushed
2 tbsp fresh thyme leaves
200 ml/7 fl oz red wine
4 tbsp sherry or balsamic vinegar
85 g/3 oz redcurrant jelly
55 g/2 oz butter, cut into chunks

top tip

Enjoy these flavourful duck breasts with simple sides such as glazed baby carrots and wilted greens.

1. Preheat the oven to 180°C/350°F/Gas Mark 4. Score the skin of each duck breast with four diagonal cuts down to the fat (but not into the meat). Season with salt and pepper. Place a large heavy-based frying pan over a high heat and add the duck breasts, skin-side down. There is no need to add any fat; the duck breasts will release plenty as they cook. Sear for about 10 minutes until the skin is crisp. Be careful, as they will spit. Turn the breasts over and sear on the other side for 2 minutes. Remove from the frying pan and put into a roasting tin. Keep warm.

2. Pour off most of the fat from the pan, reserving about a tablespoon. Put the pan over a medium heat, add the shallots and fry for 5–10 minutes until soft.

3. Meanwhile, put the duck breasts into the preheated oven and cook for about 15 minutes (this will cook the duck to pink, which is how it ought to be served). Add the garlic and thyme to the shallots and cook for a further 2 minutes. Add the wine and vinegar, simmer for 5 minutes, then stir in the redcurrant jelly and butter. When the duck is cooked, remove it from the oven, cover and keep warm for 5 minutes.

4. Cut each breast diagonally into four fat slices, lay on warmed plates and pour over the sauce.

cals: 584   fat: 29.4g   sat fat: 11.9g   fibre: 1.3g   carbs: 26.2g   sugar: 21.5g   salt: 1.2g   protein: 45g

roast gammon

prep: 20 mins, plus soaking, cooling and chilling
cook: 1½ hours, plus optional standing

1.3 kg/3 lb boneless gammon,
   pre-soaked if necessary

2 tbsp Dijon mustard

85g/3 oz demerara sugar

½ tsp ground cinnamon

½ tsp ground ginger

18 whole cloves

ready-made red current sauce,
   to serve (optional)

1. Place the gammon in a large saucepan, cover with cold water and slowly bring to the boil over a gentle heat. Cover the pan and simmer very gently for one hour.

2. Preheat the oven to 200°C/400°F/ Gas Mark 6.

3. Remove the gammon from the pan and drain. Remove the rind from the gammon and discard. Score the fat into a diamond-shaped pattern with a sharp knife.

4. Spread the mustard over the fat. Mix the sugar and the ground spices together on a plate and roll the gammon in the mixture, pressing down well to coat evenly.

5. Stud the diamond shapes with cloves and place the joint in a roasting tin. Roast in the preheated oven for 20 minutes, until the glaze is a rich golden colour.

6. To serve hot, leave to stand for 20 minutes before carving. If the gammon is to be served cold, it can be cooked a day ahead. Serve with red current sauce, if desired.

serves 6

cals: 496   fat: 30.7g   sat fat: 10.2g   fibre: 0.3g   carbs: 14.6g   sugar: 14.2g   salt: 2.9g   protein: 37.3g

cured ham cooked in cider

prep: 20 mins
cook: 8 hours, plus standing

1 kg/2 lb 4 oz boneless gammon joint
1 onion, halved
4 cloves
6 black peppercorns
1 tsp juniper berries
1 celery stick, chopped
1 carrot, sliced
1 litre/1¾ pints medium cider
salad, to serve

1. Place a trivet or rack in a slow cooker, if you like, and stand the gammon on it. Otherwise, just place the gammon in the slow cooker. Stud each onion half with two of the cloves and add to the slow cooker with the peppercorns, juniper berries, celery and carrot.

2. Pour in the cider, cover and cook on low for 8 hours, until the meat is tender.

3. Remove the gammon from the cooker and place on a board. Tent with foil and leave to stand for 10–15 minutes. Discard the cooking liquid and flavourings.

4. Remove any rind and fat from the gammon joint and then carve into slices. Transfer to serving plates and serve immediately with a salad.

top tip

This cured ham is also scrumptious served in sandwiches — stuff the ham between slices of fresh bread, spread with butter and mustard.

cals: 252   fat: 7.5g   sat fat: 2.5g   fibre: trace   carbs: 0g   sugar: 0g   salt: 2.9g   protein: 43.4g

roast venison with brandy sauce

prep: 15–20 mins
cook: 1 hour 50 mins–1 hour 55 mins

6 tbsp vegetable oil
1.7 kg/3 lb 12 oz saddle of
   venison, trimmed
salt and pepper
fresh thyme sprigs, to garnish
roast potatoes, to serve (optional)

brandy sauce
1 tbsp plain flour
4 tbsp vegetable stock
175 ml/6 fl oz brandy
100 ml/3½ fl oz double cream

top tip

Roast parsnips and some seasonal green veg are all you need to complete this sensational meal, perfect for a celebration or special occasion.

1. Preheat the oven to 180°C/350°F/Gas Mark 4.

2. Heat half the oil in a frying pan over a high heat. Season the venison to taste with salt and pepper, add to the pan and cook until lightly browned all over. Pour the remaining oil into a roasting pan. Add the venison, cover with foil and roast in the oven, basting occasionally, for 1½ hours, or until cooked through. Remove from the oven and transfer to a warmed serving platter. Cover with foil and set aside.

3. To make the sauce, stir the flour into the roasting pan over the hob and cook for 1 minute. Pour in the stock and heat it, stirring to loosen the sediment from the base. Gradually stir in the brandy and bring to the boil, then reduce the heat and simmer, stirring, for 10–15 minutes until the sauce has thickened a little. Remove from the heat and stir in the cream.

4. Garnish the venison with thyme and serve with the brandy sauce and roast potatoes, if desired.

cals: 683   fat: 38.2g   sat fat: 12g   fibre: 0.2g   carbs: 3.8g   sugar: 0.5g   salt: 1.6g   protein: 54.8g

carving your meat

Smaller game birds are often served whole or halved. The same basic techniques for carving apply to chicken and most other birds as follows:

- Remove the legs.
- Remove the wings.
- Carve the meat from the breast, slicing downwards, with the knife running parallel to the bird.
- Remove any remaining meat from the carcass, including the oysters – the nugget of flesh either side of the bird on the underside – by hand. The technique of carving the breast meat can vary to accommodate the size and shape of the bird, as follows:

Duck
Remove the legs and wings and slice the meat from the neck end. Slice close to the breastbone and loosen the breast meat before carving the first slice. Holding the knife at a 45-degree angle, cut the remaining breast meat parallel to the first slice.

Goose
Remove the legs and wings and slice the meat from the neck end. Carve long, thick slices of meat along the length of the breast, holding the knife almost flat against the meat.

Turkey
Remove the wings and legs. Carve the dark meat from the legs, holding the knuckle end of the leg and cutting downwards. Carve the breast into thick slices downwards from the fattest part of the breast on either side of the breastbone.

roast pork with crackling

prep: 15–20 mins
cook: 1 hour 40 mins–2 hours, plus resting

1 piece of loin of pork, weighing
 1 kg/2 lb 4 oz, boned, and the
 rind removed and reserved

2 tbsp mustard

salt and pepper

apple sauce, to serve (optional)

top tip

Alongside a dollop of apple sauce,
crunchy roast potato wedges and braised
red cabbage are ideal accompaniments
for this popular joint

1. Preheat the oven to 200°C/400°F/Gas Mark 6.

2. Thoroughly score the pork rind with a sharp knife and sprinkle with salt. Place it on a wire rack on a baking tray and roast in the oven for 30–40 minutes until the crackling is golden brown and crisp.

3. Season the pork well with salt and pepper and spread the fat with the mustard. Place in a roasting tin and roast in the centre of the oven for 20 minutes. Reduce the oven temperature to 190°C/375°F/Gas Mark 5 and cook for a further 50–60 minutes until the meat is a good colour and the juices run clear when it is pierced with a skewer.

4. Remove the meat from the oven and place on a warmed serving plate, cover with foil and leave in a warm place for 10 minutes.

5. Carve the pork into slices and serve on warmed plates with pieces of the crackling. Best served with apple sauce, if desired.

serves 4

cals: 530   fat: 24.5g   sat fat: 9.2g   fibre: 0.3g   carbs: 0.6g   sugar: 0g   salt: 2g   protein: 75.1g

roast beef & yorkshire pudding

prep: 25 mins
cook: 1 hour 55 mins, plus resting

3-kg/6 lb 8-oz joint of well-hung
   rib of beef on the bone

olive oil

salt and pepper

yorkshire pudding
250 g/9 oz plain flour, sifted

6 eggs

½ tsp salt

600 ml/1 pint milk

to serve (optional)
roast potatoes

gravy

freshly cooked seasonal vegetables

top tip

To ensure a really good rise, make sure the oil is very hot before pouring in the Yorkshire pudding batter (and don't be tempted to open the oven door while it cooks!).

1. To make the Yorkshire pudding, mix the flour, eggs and salt together in a bowl, then gradually add the milk as you beat with a whisk. When smooth set aside but don't chill.

2. Preheat the oven to 220°C/425°F/Gas Mark 7. Put a 40 x 25-cm/16 x 10-inch roasting tin in the bottom of the oven to warm for the Yorkshire pudding.

3. Rub a generous amount of olive oil and salt and pepper into the beef, then place in a roasting tin. Transfer to the preheated oven and roast for 30 minutes.

4. Reduce the temperature to 160°C/325°F/Gas Mark 3 and roast the beef for 1 hour. Remove the beef from the oven and increase the temperature to 220°C/425°F/Gas Mark 7. Cover the beef with foil and leave to rest for at least 30 minutes.

5. Remove the roasting tin from the bottom of the oven and add some oil. Put it back in the oven for 5 minutes, then remove it and add the Yorkshire pudding batter. Put it back in the hot oven for about 20 minutes.

6. Remove the Yorkshire pudding from the oven. Cut the rib bones off the meat and carve the beef.

7. Serve with the Yorkshire pudding. Can be served with roast potatoes, gravy and vegetables, if desired.

serves 8

cals: 954   fat: 68g   sat fat: 25.9g   fibre: 0.8g   carbs: 27.8g   sugar: 4g   salt: 1.3g   protein: 53.7g

garlic-crusted roast haddock

prep: 20 mins
cook: 25-27 mins

900 g/2 lb floury potatoes

125 ml/4 fl oz milk

55 g/2 oz butter

4 haddock fillets, about 225 g/8 oz
each

1 tbsp sunflower oil

4 garlic cloves, finely chopped

salt and pepper

2 tbsp chopped fresh parsley,
to garnish

top tip

Be careful not to over-cook the fish. Translucent raw fish like haddock becomes opaque and firm to the touch once cooked.

1. Preheat the oven to 230°C/450°F/Gas Mark 8.

2. Cut the potatoes into chunks and cook in a saucepan of lightly salted water for 15 minutes, or until tender. Drain well. Mash in the saucepan until smooth. Set over a low heat and beat in the milk, butter and salt and pepper to taste.

3. Put the haddock fillets in a roasting tin and brush the fish with the oil. Sprinkle the garlic on top, add salt and pepper to taste, then spread with the mashed potatoes. Roast in the oven for 8–10 minutes, or until the fish is just tender.

4. Meanwhile, preheat the grill. Transfer the fish to the grill and cook for about 2 minutes, or until golden brown. Sprinkle with the chopped parsley and serve immediately.

serves 4

cals: 510   fat: 16.4g   sat fat: 8.1g   fibre: 4.7g   carbs: 47.8g   sugar: 3.5g   salt: 2.9g   protein: 42g

roast salmon with lemon & herbs

6 tbsp extra virgin olive oil

1 onion, sliced

1 leek, trimmed and sliced

juice of ½ lemon

2 tbsp chopped fresh parsley

2 tbsp chopped fresh dill

500 g/1 lb 2 oz salmon fillets

salt and pepper

freshly cooked baby spinach leaves
   and lemon wedges, to serve
   (optional)

top tip

There are two types of parsley — curly and flat-leaf. Either can be used in this recipe; the flat-leaf variety tends to have a slightly more robust flavour.

1. Preheat the oven to 200°C/400°F/Gas Mark 6. Heat 1 tablespoon of the oil in a frying pan over a medium heat. Add the onion and leek and cook, stirring, for about 4 minutes until slightly soft.

2. Meanwhile, put the remaining oil in a small bowl with the lemon juice and herbs, and season. Stir together well. Rinse the fish under cold running water, then pat dry with kitchen paper. Arrange the fish in a shallow, ovenproof baking dish.

3. Remove the frying pan from the heat and spread the onion and leek over the fish. Pour the oil mixture over the top, ensuring that everything is well coated. Roast in the centre of the preheated oven for about 10 minutes or until the fish is cooked through.

4. Arrange the cooked spinach on warmed serving plates. Remove the fish and vegetables from the oven and serve immediately with cooked spinach and lemon wedges, if desired.

serves 4

cals: 471   fat: 37.3g   sat fat: 6.6g   fibre: 1.1g   carbs: 7.4g   sugar: 2.6g   salt: 1.7g   protein: 26.3g

pot roasted leg of lamb

prep: 25-30 mins
cook: 2 hours 25 mins-3 hours

1 leg of lamb, weighing 1.6 kg/3 lb 8 oz

3–4 fresh rosemary sprigs

115 g/4 oz streaky bacon rashers

4 tbsp olive oil

2–3 garlic cloves, crushed

2 onions, sliced

2 carrots, sliced

2 celery sticks, sliced

300 ml/10 fl oz dry white wine

1 tbsp tomato purée

300 ml/10 fl oz lamb or chicken stock

3 medium tomatoes, peeled, quartered
   and deseeded

1 tbsp chopped fresh parsley

1 tbsp chopped fresh oregano or
   marjoram

salt and pepper

fresh rosemary sprigs, to garnish

1. Wipe the lamb all over with kitchen paper, trim off any excess fat and season to taste with salt and pepper, rubbing well in. Lay the sprigs of rosemary over the lamb, cover evenly with the bacon rashers and tie securely in place with kitchen string.

2. Heat the oil in a frying pan and fry the lamb over a medium heat for 10 minutes, turning several times. Remove from the pan.

3. Preheat the oven to 160°C/325°F/Gas Mark 3. Transfer the oil from the frying pan to a large flameproof casserole and cook the garlic and onions for 3–4 minutes until the onions are beginning to soften. Add the carrots and celery and cook for a further few minutes.

4. Lay the lamb on top of the vegetables and press down to partly submerge. Pour the wine over the lamb, add the tomato purée and simmer for 3–4 minutes. Add the stock, tomatoes and herbs and season to taste with salt and pepper. Return to the boil for a further 3–4 minutes.

5. Cover the casserole tightly and cook in the oven for 2–2½ hours until very tender.

6. Remove the lamb from the casserole and, if you like, remove the bacon and herbs together with the string. Keep the lamb warm. Strain the juices, skimming off any excess fat, and serve in a jug. The vegetables may be put around the joint or in a dish. Garnish with sprigs of rosemary.

serves 4

cals: 851   fat: 47.3g   sat fat: 16.4g   fibre: 3.7g   carbs: 18.9g   sugar: 10.5g   salt: 2g   protein: 72.5g

roast sea bass

prep: 30 mins
cook: 35-40 mins

1.3–1.8 kg/3–4 lb whole sea bass, gutted

1 small onion, finely chopped

2 garlic cloves, finely chopped

2 tbsp finely chopped fresh herbs, such as parsley, chervil and tarragon

25 g/1 oz anchovy fillets, finely chopped

25 g/1 oz butter

150 ml/5 fl oz white wine

2 tbsp crème fraîche

salt and pepper

top tip

For a fabulous family supper, boiled or crushed new potatoes and seasonal fresh vegetables or a garden salad will finish this off perfectly.

1. Preheat the oven to 200°C/400°F/Gas Mark 6.

2. Remove any scales from the fish and clean it thoroughly both inside and out. If desired, trim off the fins with a pair of scissors. Using a sharp knife, make five or six cuts diagonally into the flesh of the fish on both sides. Season well with salt and pepper, both inside and out.

3. Mix the onion, garlic, herbs and anchovies together in a bowl.

4. Stuff the fish with half the mixture and spoon the remainder into a roasting tin. Place the sea bass on top.

5. Spread the butter over the sea bass, pour over the wine and place in the oven. Roast for 30–35 minutes until the fish is cooked through.

6. Remove the fish from the tin to a warmed serving dish. Return the tin to the top of the stove and stir the onion mixture and juices together over a medium heat. Add the crème fraîche and pour into a warmed serving bowl.

7. Serve the sea bass whole and divide at the table. Spoon a little sauce on the side.

serves 4

cals: 318   fat: 12g   sat fat: 6g   fibre: 0.6g   carbs: 5.1g   sugar: 2.8g   salt: 1.8g   protein: 39.4g

beef wellington

prep: 35–40 mins, plus cooling and chilling
cook: 1 hour 5 mins–1 hour 20 mins

2 tbsp olive oil or vegetable oil

1.5 kg/3 lb 5 oz beef fillet, cut from the middle of the fillet, trimmed of fat and sinew

55 g/2 oz butter

150 g/5½ oz mushrooms, chopped

2 garlic cloves, crushed

150 g/5½ oz smooth liver pâté

few drops of truffle oil (optional)

1 tbsp fresh parsley, finely chopped

2 tsp English mustard

500 g/1 lb 2 oz ready-made puff pastry

1 egg, lightly beaten

salt and pepper

top tip

Fillet is a very tender, prime cut of beef with a good flavour, making it ideal for this special occasion recipe.

1. Place a large frying pan over a high heat and add the olive oil. Rub salt and pepper into the beef and sear in the pan. (This method gives a rare version. If you want it less rare, roast it at 220°C/425°F/Gas Mark 7 for 20 minutes at this stage.) Set aside to cool.

2. Heat the butter in a frying pan over a medium heat, add the mushrooms and fry for 5 minutes. Reduce the heat, add the garlic and fry for another 5 minutes. Put the mushrooms and garlic in a bowl, add the pâté, truffle oil, if using, and parsley, and beat with a fork. Leave to cool.

3. Rub the mustard into the seared beef fillet. Roll out the pastry into a rectangle large enough to wrap the whole fillet with some to spare. Spread the mushroom paste in the middle of the pastry in a shape the size of the base of the beef and lay the beef on top. Brush the edges of the pastry with beaten egg and fold it over, edges overlapping, and across the meat to enclose it completely.

4. Preheat the oven to 225°C/425°F/Gas Mark 7. With the join underneath, place the wrapped beef in a roasting tin and brush with beaten egg. Leave to chill in the refrigerator for 15 minutes, then transfer to the preheated oven and bake for 50 minutes. Check after 30 minutes – if the pastry looks golden brown, cover it in foil to prevent it burning. Remove from the oven, cut into thick slices and serve.

serves 6

cals: 890   fat: 52.1g   sat fat: 24g   fibre: 2g   carbs: 31.9g   sugar: 1.1g   salt: 2.6g   protein: 72.9.g

Ribs smothered in a sticky sauce, whether cooked on the barbecue, in the oven or under the grill are always fun, mostly because you can eat them with your fingers and pretend to be a child. But don't get carried away and forget your chops and other cuts, there are plenty to choose from.

a meating of minds

pork spare ribs

prep: 25 mins, plus chilling
cook: 2 hours–2 hours 40 mins, plus standing

1 rack pork spare ribs, weighing
   1.8–2.25 kg/4–5 lb
1 onion, peeled and quartered
2 bay leaves
2 tsp whole black peppercorns
1 tsp salt
ready-made barbecue sauce

1. This recipe requires a barbecue. Place the ribs in a large saucepan (cut the rack in half, if necessary) and cover with cold water. Add the onion, bay leaves, peppercorns and salt and bring to the boil over a high heat. Reduce the heat to low and simmer for 1½–2 hours, testing occasionally during the last 30 minutes of cooking. Remove from the heat once the meat begins to pull apart with little resistance. Drain the ribs, discarding the onion, peppercorns and bay leaves.

2. Coat the ribs with some of the barbecue sauce, then cover and refrigerate for 2–8 hours. Remove from the refrigerator 30 minutes before you are ready to start grilling.

3. Meanwhile, preheat the barbecue to high. Baste the ribs with more barbecue sauce, place on the barbecue rack and cook over a high heat for 12–15 minutes on each side, turning and basting every 5–10 minutes, until the sauce is caramelized and just beginning to blacken in places.

4. Remove from the heat and leave to stand for 5 minutes. Cut into individual ribs and serve, brushed with some of the sauce.

top tip

Serve these finger-licking ribs with ample napkins and finger bowls to hand (though some finger-licking and lip-smacking is compulsory!).

chilli-flavoured
spare ribs

prep: 15 mins, plus marinating
cook: 1-1½ hours

1.8–2.25 kg/4–5 lb pork spare ribs

smoky rub

2 tbsp mild chilli powder

2 tsp smoked paprika

2 tsp mild paprika

4 tsp dried oregano

2 tsp onion powder

2 tsp salt

mashed potato and greens, to serve
  (optional)

top tip

Try using the smoky rub on other cuts
of pork, beef or lamb, such as joints,
chops or steaks.

1. To make the smoky rub, combine the chilli powder, smoked paprika, mild paprika, oregano, onion powder and salt in a small bowl. Rub the mixture all over the ribs and set aside for 15 minutes to marinate.

2. Preheat the oven to 160°C/325°F/Gas Mark 3 and line a roasting tin with foil. Put a rack in the roasting tin. Place the ribs on the rack and roast for 1-1½ hours, or until cooked through and the meat is tender.

3. Remove the ribs from the oven, cut into serving portions and serve with mashed potato and spring greens, if desired.

serves 4

cals: 935   fat: 68.4g   sat fat: 34g   fibre: 3.1g   carbs: 5.4g   sugar: 0.6g   salt: 1.5g   protein: 75.4g

rack of lamb

prep: 15–20 mins
cook: 45 mins–1 hour 5 mins, plus standing

1 trimmed rack of lamb,
   weighing 500 g/1 lb 2oz
salt and pepper

sauce
1 tbsp extra virgin olive oil
1 small onion, finely chopped
1 garlic clove, crushed
1–2 tbsp redcurrant jelly
1 tbsp soy sauce
200 ml/7 fl oz blood orange or orange
   juice
150 ml/5 fl oz red wine
1 fresh rosemary sprig
salt and pepper

top tip
Superb for a sharing supper for two, serve this prime cut of lamb with crushed new potatoes and seasonal fresh greens.

1. To make the sauce, heat the oil in a small saucepan. Add the onion and garlic and cook for 3 minutes, stirring occasionally. Add the redcurrant jelly, soy sauce, blood orange juice, wine and rosemary and bring to the boil, stirring until the jelly has dissolved. Reduce the heat and simmer for 20 minutes, or until the sauce has reduced by half and is slightly syrupy. Season to taste with salt and pepper.

2. Preheat the oven to 200°C/400°F/ Gas Mark 6. Season the meat lightly with salt and pepper and sear on all sides in a hot frying pan. Transfer the meat to a roasting pan and brush with some of the sauce. Roast in the preheated oven for 8 minutes for medium-rare, 15 minutes for medium and 20–25 minutes for well done. Remove the meat from the oven and transfer to a board. Cover loosely with foil and leave to stand for 10 minutes.

3. Meanwhile strain the sauce and reheat. Slice the rack through into individual chops and arrange on serving plates. Drizzle with the sauce and serve immediately.

serves 2

cals: 815   fat: 19.5g   sat fat: 20.4g   fibre: 1.6g   carbs: 28g   sugar: 21.3g   salt: 5.2g   protein: 45.3g

spicy baby back ribs

prep: 15-20 mins, plus marinating
cook: 4 hours

4 baby back pork ribs, each weighing
    500 g/1lb 2 oz

spicy marinade
2 tbsp soft brown sugar
3 tbsp Old Bay seasoning
1 tbsp Worcestershire sauce
4 tsp salt

apple glaze
150 ml/5 fl oz apple juice
2 tbsp olive oil
2 tbsp cider vinegar

top tip

Worcestershire sauce adds a robust, spicy
flavour to the marinade, ideal for these
pork ribs. Try using the marinade for
other cuts of pork like steaks and chops.

1. This recipe requires a barbecue. To make the spicy marinade, mix together all the ingredients in a large bowl then add the pork ribs and turn to coat thoroughly.

2. Lay the ribs in a non-metallic dish, adding any remaining marinade from the bowl. Cover the dish with clingfilm and place in the refrigerator for at least 12 hours to marinate.

3. Remove the ribs from the refrigerator for at least an hour before you want to cook them. This will allow them to come back up to room temperature.

4. To make the apple glaze, mix together the apple juice, olive oil and cider vinegar in a small bowl and set aside.

5. Prepare the barbecue for indirect cooking and preheat to medium-low.

6. Cook the ribs on the barbecue grill for 4 hours, with the lid on. Brush the ribs on each side with the apple glaze every 30 minutes.

7. When cooked through and the meat is falling off the bone, remove from the barbecue. Check that the centre of the meat is not pink and the juices run clear, then serve immediately.

cals: 748   fat: 64.5g   sat fat: 23.4g   fibre: trace   carbs: 12.8g   sugar: 11.9g   salt: 8.8g   protein: 67.6g

chicken wings with
hot sauce

prep: 25 mins
cook: 45-55 mins, plus resting

1.8 kg/4 lb chicken wings,
   thawed if frozen, and patted dry

1 tbsp vegetable oil

1 tbsp plain flour

1 tsp salt

ready-made blue cheese dressing,
   to serve (optional)

hot sauce

150 ml/5 fl oz hot red cayenne pepper
   sauce

115 g/4 oz cold unsalted butter,
   cut into 2.5-cm/1-inch slices

1½ tbsp white vinegar

¼ tsp Worcestershire sauce

1 tsp Tabasco

¼ tsp cayenne pepper

pinch of garlic powder

salt to taste

top tip

Chicken wings are economical to buy as they are bony and quite fatty, but they are great for roasting, barbecuing and deep-frying, jazzed up with marinades, sauces or dips.

1. Preheat the oven to 220°C/425°F/Gas Mark 7. 2. If using whole wings, cut each into two pieces. Toss the wings with the oil, flour and salt until evenly coated.

3. Line two baking trays with lightly greased foil or silicone baking mats. Divide the wings between the trays and spread them out. Bake in the preheated oven for 25 minutes.

4. Meanwhile, mix all the sauce ingredients in a saucepan. Bring to a simmer, whisking, over a medium heat. Remove from the heat and set aside. Taste and adjust the seasoning and spices, if necessary.

5. Remove the chicken wings from the oven, turn the wings over, then return them to the oven and cook for a further 20–30 minutes, depending on the size of the wings, until well browned and cooked through. When fully cooked the juices will run clear when a skewer is inserted into the thickest part of the meat. Transfer to a large mixing bowl.

6. Pour the warm sauce over the hot wings and toss with a spoon or palette knife to completely coat. Leave to rest for 5 minutes. Before serving, toss again and serve with blue cheese dressing, if desired.

serves 2

cals: 2198   fat: 161.6g   sat fat: 61.4g   fibre: 2.7g   carbs: 30g   sugar: 20.4g   salt: 7.3g   protein: 156.2g

lamb chops with tomato-mint jam

prep: 25 mins, plus marinating
cook: 55 mins

8 lamb loin chops or 4 lamb shoulder chops, about 2–2.5 cm/¾–1 inch thick

salt and pepper

marinade

4 tbsp olive oil

4 tbsp red wine vinegar

2 garlic cloves, finely chopped

tomato-mint jam

2 tbsp olive oil

1 small onion, diced

450 g/1 lb plum tomatoes, peeled, deseeded and chopped

1–2 jalapeño chillies or bird's eye chillies, deseeded and finely chopped

100 g/3½ oz sugar

juice of 1 lemon

½ tsp salt

2 tbsp chopped fresh mint leaves, plus extra to garnish

1. This recipe requires a barbecue. To make the marinade, combine the oil, vinegar and garlic in a baking dish or bowl large enough to hold all of the chops. Season the chops to taste with salt and pepper and add them to the marinade, turning to coat. Cover and leave to marinate in the refrigerator for 2–8 hours.

2. To make the jam, heat the oil over a medium-high heat in a large, heavy-based frying pan. Add the onion and cook, stirring, for about 5 minutes, until it begins to soften. Add the tomatoes, chillies, sugar, lemon juice and salt and bring to the boil. Reduce the heat to medium-low and simmer, stirring occasionally, for about 45 minutes, until the tomatoes have broken down and the jam becomes thick. Stir in the mint, remove from the heat and set aside.

3. Meanwhile, preheat the barbecue to high. Place the chops on the barbecue rack and cook to taste, about 5–7 minutes on each side for medium. Serve immediately with the tomato-mint jam and garnished with mint.

top tip

Oval plum tomatoes are ideal for cooking in recipes such as this. Choose ripe tomatoes for the best, sweet flavour.

prime rib of beef

prep: 20 mins, plus chilling and standing
cook: 2 hours 20 mins, plus resting

4 kg/9 lb rib of beef on the bone, trimmed and tied

2½ tbsp softened butter (or ½ tbsp per rib bone)

salt and pepper

horseradish sauce

6 tbsp creamed horseradish

6 tbsp soured cream

1. To make the sauce, mix the horseradish and soured cream together in a small bowl. Cover with clingfilm and chill until required.

2. Place the beef in a large roasting tin. Rub the entire surface of the meat with butter and season generously with salt and pepper. Leave to stand at room temperature for 2 hours.

3. Meanwhile, preheat the oven to 230°C/450°F/Gas Mark 8. Put the meat in the preheated oven and roast for 20 minutes to seal the outside. Then reduce the oven temperature to 160°C/325°F/Gas Mark 3 and roast for 2 hours, until the temperature of the meat reaches 43–46°C/110–115°F when tested with a meat thermometer, for medium-rare, or until cooked to your liking.

4. Set aside to rest for 30 minutes before serving. While resting the meat will continue to cook – for medium-rare the final internal temperature will be approximately 54–57°C/130–135°F. Slice and serve with the horseradish sauce.

top tip

Yorkshire pudding, seasonal veg and gravy are perfect for this traditional roast joint

cals: 1116   fat: 88.4g   sat fat: 40.5g   fibre: 0.5g   carbs: 5g   sugar: 3.9g   salt: 2.2g   protein: 75.9g

chilli lamb cutlets

prep: 20 mins
cook: 14-17 mins, plus resting

60 g/2¼ oz fresh parsley leaves
2 garlic cloves
juice of 1 lemon
1–2 red chillies or green chillies
1 tbsp sweet paprika
4 tbsp olive oil
4 x 5-cm/2-inch thick lamb cutlets
salt and pepper
pittas, to serve

salad
1 cucumber
1 tbsp fresh parsley leaves
225 g/8 oz cherry tomatoes
juice of 1 lemon
½ tsp salt

top tip

If you can, buy whole spices in small quantities and grind them fresh each time to enjoy their finest flavour.

1. Put the parsley, garlic, lemon juice, chillies, paprika and 1 teaspoon of salt into a food processor and process until smooth. Add the oil and process to combine. Season the lamb with salt and pepper, then coat them on both sides with some of the sauce. Reserve the remaining sauce.

2. To make the salad, dice the cucumber, finely chop the parsley and halve the tomatoes, then put them all into a medium-sized bowl. Toss with the lemon juice and salt and set aside until ready to serve.

3. Heat a ridged griddle pan over a medium-high heat. Add the chops and cook for about 6 minutes on each side for medium-rare, or a bit longer for medium. Remove from the heat and leave to rest for a few minutes before serving. Meanwhile, warm the bread under the grill. Serve the chops with the bread, salad and reserved sauce.

serves 4

cals: 514   fat: 39.6g   sat fat: 13.6g   fibre: 2.5g   carbs: 9.9g   sugar: 4g   salt: 1.9g   protein: 28g

piri piri chicken

prep: 15-20 mins
cook: 20-25 mins

8 chicken drumsticks
1½ tsp crushed dried red chillies
2 garlic cloves, crushed
1 tsp dried oregano
2 tsp smoked paprika
juice of ½ lemon
salt and pepper

to serve (optional)
lemon wedges
mixed salad leaves
tortillas

top tip

Smoked paprika adds lovely flavour and warmth to the spice mixture in this popular Portuguese chicken dish. It's also fantastic in marinades and rubs.

1. Preheat the oven to 220°C/425°F/Gas Mark 7. Cut deep slashes into the thickest parts of the meat.

2. Place the chillies, garlic, oregano, paprika and lemon juice in a large mixing bowl. Season to taste with salt and pepper and mix together. Add the chicken and turn to coat evenly.

3. Arrange the chicken in a single layer in a large, shallow roasting tin. Bake in the preheated oven for 20–25 minutes, turning occasionally. Check the chicken is tender and the juices run clear when a skewer is inserted into the thickest part of the meat.

4. Serve with lemon wedges, mixed salad and tortillas, if desired.

serves 4

cals: 236 fat: 11.8g sat fat: 3.2g fibre: 1.3g carbs: 2.8g sugar: 0.4g salt: 2.1 protein: 28.4g

A. Fore Rib

Also known as best rib and one of the most expensive cuts of beef. Sold as a joint on the bone or as a boneless rolled joint. Ideal for roasting; also suitable for braising. Single rib cutlets are also available and are suitable for grilling, frying and barbecuing.

Prime rib is cut from below the fore rib. One of the most expensive cuts and one of the largest roasting joints. Should be chined to make carving easier. Also sold boned and sliced as rib-eye steaks for frying, grilling and barbecuing.

B. Chuck & Blade

Often sold as braising, chuck or blade steak. Sold ready-cubed or as slices. Requires long, slow, moist cooking, so is therefore suitable for braising, stewing and casseroling, or for use in pies. Blade steaks may also be available and are suitable for grilling or frying.

C. Neck & Clod

Neck is usually sold as stewing steak or mince and is one of the most inexpensive cuts of beef. Clod is a similar cut. Requires long, slow, moist cooking, so is therefore suitable for braising, stewing and casseroling.

D. Thick Rib

Also known as top rib. Usually sold as a boneless, rolled joint or as steaks for pot-roasting or braising.

E. Brisket

Sold as a joint on the bone or as a boneless rolled joint and is an inexpensive cut. Sometimes sold salted for boiling. Tends to be quite fatty. Requires long, slow, moist cooking so is suitable for pot-roasting, braising, stewing and boiling (if salted).

F. Shin

Sold with or without the bone. Requires long, slow, moist cooking so is suitable for stewing, casseroling or braising.

G. Thin Rib

This is usually sold boned and rolled or as short ribs (with bones left in). Suitable for casseroling, stewing, braising or pot-roasting.

H. Sirloin

Prime, tender and juicy roasting joint marbled with fat, either sold on the bone or as a boneless rolled joint. Several steaks are cut from the sirloin including entrecôte, sirloin, T-bone, fillet, porterhouse and minute. Joints suitable for roasting; steaks suitable for grilling, griddling, frying, barbecuing and stir-frying. Fillet steak or tenderloin is lean and tender. Steaks suitable for grilling, griddling, frying, barbecuing, stir-frying; whole fillet suitable for roasting or wrapping in pastry and baking. Also used to make carpaccio or steak tartare.

I. Flank

This cut can be fatty. Often made into mince rather than sold as a piece. Suitable for stewing and braising, or it can be thinly sliced, marinated and stir-fried.

J. Leg

Can be sold as braising steak or stewing steak. Sold ready-cubed or as slices. Requires long, slow, moist cooking, so is therefore suitable for braising, stewing and casseroling.

K. Thick flank

Also known as top rump and sometimes sold as braising steak. Suitable for pot-roasting, braising, casseroling and stewing

L. Topside

Suitable for roasting, braising, casseroling, pot-roasting or stir-frying. Also good cubed and used in pies or for kebabs. Thinly sliced topside steaks are also available.

M. Silverside

Very lean, boneless joint traditionally sold salted or cured for boiling as salt beef, but also sold unsalted for roasting and barded with fat. Suitable for roasting, braising, pot-roasting or boiling (if salted/cured).

N. Rump

Lean and tender cut of beef with a narrow edge of fat (not as tender as sirloin and much less tender than fillet). Suitable for grilling, griddling, frying, barbecuing, stir-frying and kebabs, and braising in casseroles.

turkey drumsticks with mexican spice rub

prep: 10-15 mins, plus marinating
cook: 40 mins, plus resting

4 turkey drumsticks, each weighing
500 g/1 lb 2 oz

mexican rub

2 tbsp soft brown sugar

2 tbsp olive oil

zest and juice of 1 orange

1 tbsp salt

1 tbsp paprika

1 tsp pepper

1 tsp garlic granules

1 tbsp chipotle purée

1 tbsp ground cumin

1 tsp dried oregano

1 tsp dried thyme

1. This recipe requires a barbecue. To make the rub, mix all of the ingredients in a large bowl. Add the turkey drumsticks, turning a few times to coat thoroughly.

2. Cover with clingfilm and place in the refrigerator for at least 2 hours. Remove from the refrigerator for at least an hour before you want to cook them.

3. Prepare the barbecue for indirect cooking and preheat to medium.

4. Place the turkey on the barbecue grill and cook for 40 minutes with the lid on. Check the turkey is tender and the juices run clear when a skewer is inserted into the thickest part of the meat.

5. Cover with foil and leave to rest.

top tip

Store dried herbs and spices in airtight containers in a cool, dark, dry place. Replace them every 6 months as they deteriorate quickly, losing their fresh flavour.

cals: 824   fat: 42.9g   sat fat: 12g   fibre: 1.7g   carbs: 13.3g   sugar: 9.9g   salt: 5.2g   protein: 98g

chicken breasts with green olive tapenade

prep: 20 mins, plus marinating
cook: 14–16 mins

4 skinless, boneless chicken breasts
salt and pepper

marinade
4 tbsp olive oil
juice of 1 lemon
1 garlic clove, finely chopped
1 tbsp finely chopped fresh rosemary

green olive tapenade
1 garlic clove
200 g/7 oz stoned green olives
1 tbsp capers, rinsed and drained
1 tbsp chopped fresh flat-leaf parsley
zest and juice of 1 lemon
4 tbsp olive oil
55 g/2 oz toasted pine nuts

1. This recipe requires a barbecue. To make the marinade, combine the oil, lemon juice, garlic and rosemary in a bowl large enough to hold the chicken. Season the chicken with salt and pepper and add to the marinade. Toss to coat, cover and refrigerate for at least 30 minutes and up to 8 hours.

2. To make the tapenade, put the garlic, olives, capers and parsley in a food processor and process until chopped. Add the lemon zest and juice and oil and process to a smooth paste. Add the pine nuts and pulse until they are coarsely chopped. Preheat the barbecue to medium-high.

3. Place the chicken breasts on the barbecue rack over a medium-high heat and cook for about 7–8 minutes on each side, or until the chicken is tender and the juices run clear when a skewer is inserted into the thickest part of the meat. Serve immediately, topped with some of the tapenade.

top tip

Tapenade is also great served as a spread on bread or with crudités. Or, try stirring a little into pasta sauces or casseroles.

lamb roasted with lemon & thyme

1 leg of lamb, weighing 2.5–3 kg/
   5 lb 8 oz–6 lb 8 oz
250 ml/9 fl oz chicken stock
250 ml/9 fl oz red wine
1 tbsp redcurrant jelly
seasonal vegetables and mint sauce,
   to serve, to serve (optional)

marinade
1 bulb of garlic, cloves separated but
   unpeeled
5 lemons or blood oranges
1 tbsp fresh rosemary leaves, chopped
1 tbsp fresh thyme leaves
2 tbsp salt

top tip

The zingy lemons in the marinade add flavour and help to tenderize the meat. The strong, aromatic flavour of fresh thyme is popular in Mediterranean-style dishes.

1. Remove the lamb from the refrigerator and pat dry with kitchen paper. Combine all the marinade ingredients in a food processor and blend to a paste.

2. Place the lamb in a roasting pan and cover with the paste so that it is completely encased. Cover loosely with foil and set aside in a cool place for an hour (or preferably in the refrigerator overnight). If the lamb has been in the refrigerator, remove it 30 minutes before cooking. Preheat the oven to 200°C/400°F/Gas Mark 6. Put the foil-covered lamb into the oven and cook for 1¾ hours.

3. Remove from the oven and remove the lamb from the roasting pan. Reserve 2 tablespoons of the marinade paste, and let the lamb rest in the foil for 15–20 minutes.

4. Meanwhile, place the roasting tin over a medium-high heat, add the marinade paste, stock, wine and jelly and simmer until reduced by about half.

5. Carve the lamb, discarding most of the paste, and serve with the gravy, vegetables and mint sauce, if desired.

cals: 628   fat: 34.6g   sat fat: 14.2g   fibre: 0.2g   carbs: 5g   sugar: 3.4g   salt: 2.8g   protein: 62.6g

beef rib cutlets with
caper & anchovy butter

prep: 20 mins
cook: 20 mins, plus resting

4 tbsp olive oil

1 tsp salt

1 tsp pepper

2 beef rib cutlets, each weighing
   800 g/1 lb 12 oz

caper & anchovy butter

5 anchovy fillets, chopped

200 g/7 oz butter, softened

2 garlic cloves, crushed

40 g/1½ oz baby capers

small bunch of parsley, chopped

1 tsp salt

1 tsp pepper

1. This recipe requires a barbecue. Place the oil, salt and pepper in a non-metallic dish large enough to fit the cutlets in. Add the cutlets and coat thoroughly. Set aside.

2. To make the butter, place all of the ingredients in a medium bowl. Beat well with a wooden spoon until well combined.

3. Prepare the barbecue for direct cooking and preheat to medium-hot.

4. Place the cutlets on the barbecue grill and cook for 10 minutes on each side for medium rare, or to your liking. Turn every now and then and brush with the butter until the cutlets are well coated.

5. When the cutlets are cooked, cover with foil and leave in a warm place to rest for 5 minutes. Serve with any remaining butter on the side.

top tip

Canned anchovy fillets add a strong, salty, piquant flavour to the butter, which combines well with capers and suits the cutlets perfectly.

cals: 1499   fat: 129g   sat fat: 58.4g   fibre: 0.7g   carbs: 1.8g   sugar: 0.g   salt: 5.6g   protein: 80.2g

sweet & sour ribs

prep: 15-20 mins
cook: 1 hour 35 mins-1 hour 50 mins

4 spring onions, finely chopped

3 tbsp lemon juice

150 ml/5 fl oz white wine vinegar

2 tsp English mustard

3 tbsp muscovado sugar

3 tbsp Worcestershire sauce

5 tbsp sun-dried tomato purée

1 kg/2 lb 4 oz pork spare ribs

salt and pepper

top tip

These classic barbecued ribs are delicious served simply with warm flatbreads or baked potatoes and a side salad or salsa.

1. This recipe requires a barbecue. Preheat the barbecue. Put the spring onions, lemon juice, vinegar, mustard, sugar, Worcestershire sauce and sun-dried tomato purée in a saucepan, season with salt and pepper and bring to the boil, stirring well to mix. Reduce the heat and simmer, stirring occasionally, for 30 minutes. Transfer the saucepan to the side of the barbecue.

2. Using a sharp knife, make deep scores all over the racks of ribs, then brush them all over with the sauce.

3. Grill over a medium barbecue, turning and brushing frequently with the sauce, for 1–1¼ hours, or until cooked through and tender. Serve immediately.

serves 4

cals: 625   fat: 42.3g   sat fat: 20.3g   fibre: 1.5g   carbs: 17.3g   sugar: 14.3g   salt: 2.8g   protein: 42g

honey-glazed pork chops

prep: 15 mins
cook: 17–21 mins

4 lean pork loin chops

4 tbsp honey

1 tbsp dry sherry

4 tbsp orange juice

2 tbsp olive oil

2.5-cm/1-inch piece fresh ginger, grated

sunflower oil, for oiling

salt and pepper

top tip

To grate fresh root ginger, peel a 2.5-cm/ 1-inch length at the end of a larger piece, then grate the peeled section holding the unpeeled ginger.

1. This recipe requires a barbecue. Preheat the barbecue. Season the pork chops with salt and pepper to taste. Reserve while you make the glaze.

2. To make the glaze, place the honey, sherry, orange juice, olive oil, and ginger in a small pan and heat gently, stirring constantly, until well blended.

3. Oil the grill rack. Cook the pork chops over hot coals for 5 minutes on each side. Brush the chops with the glaze and cook for an additional 2–4 minutes on each side, basting frequently with the glaze.

4. Transfer the pork chops to warmed serving plates and serve immediately.

serves 4

cals: 642   fat: 42g   sat fat: 13.7g   fibre: 0.2g   carbs: 19.7g   sugar: 18.6g   salt: 1.9g   protein: 46.3g

duck legs with mango relish

prep: 30 mins, plus standing
cook: 22–25 mins, plus resting

4 duck legs, about 250 g/9 oz each
4 very thin slices of lime, quartered
4 tbsp honey
juice of 1 lime
½ tsp salt
½ tsp pepper
2 tsp sesame oil, plus extra for oiling

mango relish

1 ripe mango, peeled, stoned and
finely diced
juice of 1 lime
½ small red onion, finely diced
½–1 red chilli, deseeded and
finely diced
5-cm/2-inch piece fresh ginger,
squeezed in a garlic press
6 tbsp chopped fresh coriander
1 tsp sugar
½ tsp sea salt

1. This recipe requires a barbecue. To make the relish combine all the ingredients in a serving bowl. Cover with clingfilm and leave to stand at room temperature for 1 hour to allow the flavours to develop.

2. Preheat the barbecue. Remove excess fat from the duck legs and prick the skin all over with a fork. Put in a colander and pour over a kettleful of boiling water to encourage the subcutaneous fat to flow. Pat dry with kitchen paper. Make four slashes in each leg and insert the lime segments, pushing them well in. Combine the honey, lime juice, salt, pepper and oil, mixing well. Brush the glaze all over the duck legs.

3. Oil the grill rack. Rake the coals into two heaps on either side of the barbecue and place a disposable foil drip pan in the middle. Place the duck legs skin-side down on the rack over the drip tray. Cover and cook over medium coals for 5 minutes, then turn and brush with the glaze. Continue to cook for 15 minutes, covered, turning every 5 minutes and brushing with the remaining glaze. Turn skin-side up and cook for a further 2–3 minutes for medium-rare or 4–5 minutes for medium.

4. Transfer the duck legs to a warmed serving dish. Cover with foil and leave to rest in a warm place for 10 minutes – the meat will continue to cook as it rests. Serve immediately with the relish.

marinated rack of lamb with a bean salad

prep: 25–30 mins, plus marinating
cook: 25–30 mins per 500g/1lb 2oz plus resting

2 racks of lamb with 6 ribs each, chine bones removed

salt and pepper

marinade

4 garlic cloves, crushed

4 tbsp extra virgin olive oil

4 tbsp white wine vinegar

1 tbsp smooth mustard, such as Dijon

1 tbsp clear honey

1 tsp fresh oregano leaves

1 tsp fresh thyme leaves

salad

4 tbsp olive oil

2 large tomatoes, halved, cored and coarsely chopped

2 large garlic cloves, finely chopped

400 g/14 oz canned cannellini beans or butter beans, drained and rinsed

4 spring onions, trimmed and finely chopped

1 large peeled red pepper in oil, drained and sliced

2 tbsp chopped fresh parsley

2 tbsp chopped fresh mint

squeeze of lemon juice (optional)

salt and pepper

fresh basil leaves, to garnish

1. To make the marinade, put all the ingredients in a polythene bag. Hold closed and shake to blend the ingredients. Add the racks of lamb, re-seal and shake again. Leave to marinate in the refrigerator for 4–24 hours, shaking occasionally. Remove from the refrigerator 20 minutes before cooking. Preheat the oven to 200°C/400°F/Gas Mark 6.

2. When ready to cook, remove the meat from the marinade, scrape off the herbs and pat dry. Place in a roasting tin and sprinkle the fatty surface with salt and pepper. Put the tin in the preheated oven and roast for 25 minutes per 500 g/1 lb 2 oz plus 15 minutes for medium or 30 minutes per 500 g/1 lb 2 oz plus 15 minutes for well done. Remove from the oven and leave to rest for 10 minutes before cutting into individual cutlets.

3. Meanwhile, to make the salad, heat the oil in a large frying pan over a medium heat. Add the tomatoes and garlic and stir for 3 minutes, or until the tomatoes soften and start to break down. Stir in the beans, spring onions, red pepper, parsley, mint, and salt and pepper to taste. Stir until all the ingredients are warmed through, then remove from the heat. Add a squeeze of lemon juice, if using, and adjust the seasoning.

4. Arrange the cutlets on warmed plates with the warm salad spooned over. Scatter the salad with basil leaves just before serving.

top tip

Chunks of fresh crusty bread like ciabatta are the perfect accompaniment for this flavourful Mediterranean-style dish.

serves 4

cals: 879   fat: 69.8g   sat fat: 25.7g   fibre: 6g   carbs: 14.1g   sugar: 3.7g   salt: 1.8g   protein: 46.4g

Choose your buns wisely. Most burger aficionados prefer softer buns or bread that doesn't fight with the meat or vegetable patty. If you prefer to warm your buns that is not a problem, just don't allow them to get too dry and toasty.

licence to grill

classic cheeseburgers

750 g/1 lb 10 oz fresh beef mince
1 beef stock cube
1 tbsp dried onion flakes
2 tbsp water
1–2 tbsp sunflower oil
55 g/2 oz Cheddar cheese, grated
lettuce leaves
4 burger buns, split

to serve (optional)
lettuce leaves
tomato slices
chips

1. Place the beef in a large mixing bowl. Crumble the stock cube over the meat, add the dried onion and water and mix well. Divide the meat into four portions, shape each into a ball, then flatten slightly to make a patty of your preferred thickness.

2. Place a griddle pan over a medium-high heat. Lightly brush the burgers with oil and cook for 5–6 minutes. Turn the burgers, sprinkle the cheese over the cooked side and cook for a further 5–6 minutes, or until cooked to your liking.

3. Serve with the burger buns, lettuce and tomato slices, and chips, if desired.

serves 4

top tip

Crunchy coleslaw or a dollop of
tomato ketchup or relish is all you
need to complete this family meal.

cals: 608   fat: 30.6g   sat fat: 11.5g   fibre: 1.6g   carbs: 34.3g   sugar: 3.5g   salt: 2.2g   protein: 46.8g

caramelized onion burgers

prep: 20 mins
cook: 10 mins

450 g/1 lb fresh beef mince

1 tsp salt

½ tsp pepper

½ tsp finely chopped fresh rosemary

vegetable oil, for frying

55–85 g/2–3 oz manchego cheese, grated or thinly sliced

125 ml/4 fl oz mayonnaise

4 x 15-cm/6-inch square pieces focaccia, split

to serve
caramelized onions
cos lettuce leaves
tomato slices

1. Place the beef in a medium-sized bowl with the salt, pepper and rosemary and gently mix to combine, then divide into four equal-sized portions and shape each portion into a patty.

2. Place a large frying pan or ridged griddle pan over a medium-high heat. Add enough oil to coat the base of the pan. Add the patties and cook for about 4 minutes, without moving, until the burgers are brown and release easily from the pan. Turn and cook for 2 minutes, then place some cheese on top of each burger and cook for a further 2 minutes, or until cooked to your liking.

3. Spread the mayonnaise on the focaccia and serve with the burgers. Add in caramelised onions, lettuce leaves and tomato slices.

variation

Try lamb or pork mince instead of the beef, and sun-dried tomato or olive ciabatta instead of the focaccia.

cals: 1425   fat: 73.6g   sat fat: 16.2g   fibre: 6.9g   carbs: 145.8g   sugar: 10g   salt: 6.8g   protein: 53.8g

bacon-wrapped
chicken burgers

prep: 25 mins, plus chilling
cook: 12–14 mins

450 g/1 lb fresh chicken mince
1 onion, grated
2 garlic cloves, crushed
55 g/2 oz pine nuts, toasted
55 g/2 oz Gruyère cheese, grated
2 tbsp fresh snipped chives
2 tbsp wholemeal flour
8 lean back bacon rashers
1–2 tbsp sunflower oil
salt and pepper
4 crusty rolls, split
red onion slices
lettuce leaves
4 tbsp mayonnaise
spring onions, chopped

top tip

Swap Emmenthal for the Gruyère, if you like, and for extra flavour opt for lean smoked back bacon.

1. Place the chicken mince, onion, garlic, pine nuts, Gruyère cheese, chives and salt and pepper in a food processor or blender. Using the pulse button, blend the mixture together using short sharp bursts. Scrape out onto a board and shape into four even-sized burgers. Coat in the flour, then cover and chill in the refrigerator for 1 hour.

2. Wrap each burger with two bacon rashers, securing in place with a wooden cocktail stick.

3. Heat a heavy-based frying pan over a medium heat and add the oil. When hot, add the burgers and cook over a medium heat for 5–6 minutes on each side, or until cooked through.

4. Serve the burgers in the crusty rolls with the red onion, lettuce, a spoonful of mayonnaise and spring onions. Serve immediately.

serves 4

cals: 735   fat: 41.7g   sat fat: 8.6g   fibre: 4.4g   carbs: 47.8g   sugar: 5.6g   salt: 3.9g   protein: 48.2g

barbecue burgers

450 g/1 lb fresh beef mince

1 tsp salt

½ tsp pepper

30 g/1 oz finely chopped onion

1 garlic clove, finely chopped

175 ml/6 fl oz Barbecue Sauce (see page 160)

4 soft burger buns, split

lettuce leaves and tomato slices, to serve

1. This recipe requires a barbecue. Preheat the barbecue to medium-high. Place the mince in a medium-sized bowl with the salt, pepper, onion and garlic and mix gently to combine. Divide into four equal portions and shape each portion into a patty.

2. Place 125 ml/4 fl oz of the barbecue sauce in a bowl.

3. Put the patties on the rack and cook for 4 minutes until brown on one side. Turn, baste with the barbecue sauce and cook for a further 4 minutes, or until cooked to your liking.

4. Spread some of the remaining barbecue sauce on the buns, then place the burgers in the buns. Top with lettuce leaves and tomato slices and serve immediately.

varation

Choose a Cheddar cheese to suit your taste — mild, medium, mature or extra mature will all work well.

the everything burger

prep: 20 mins
cook: 9 mins

450 g/1 lb fresh beef mince
1 tsp salt
½ tsp pepper
vegetable oil, for frying
4 Cheddar cheese slices
4 soft burger buns, split
mustard, for spreading
pickled jalapeños
coleslaw
tomato slices

1. Place the mince in a medium-sized bowl with the salt and pepper and gently mix to combine, then divide into four equal-sized portions and shape each portion into a patty.

2. Place a large frying pan or ridged griddle pan over a medium-high heat and add enough oil to coat the base of the pan. Add the patties, partially cover and cook for about 4 minutes, without moving, until the burgers are brown and release easily from the pan. Turn, place a slice of cheese on top of each burger, partially cover again and cook for a further 3 minutes, or until cooked to your liking.

3. Spread the mustard on both halves of the buns and place a few slices of pickled jalapeños on each bun base. Set a burger on top of each base, add some coleslaw and a tomato slice, and serve immediately.

variation

Swap soft wholemeal, granary or mixed seed rolls for the traditional burger buns. Choose from English, Dijon or wholegrain mustards.

cals: 499   fat: 24.4g   sat fat: 10.1g   fibre: 1.7g   carbs: 33.8g   sugar: 3.3g   salt: 3g   protein: 34.3g

turkey burgers

350 g/12 oz fresh minced turkey breast

4 tbsp fresh wholemeal breadcrumbs

1 small onion, finely chopped

1 eating apple, peeled,
   cored and finely chopped

grated rind and juice of 1 small lemon

2 tbsp finely chopped fresh parsley

sunflower oil, for brushing

salt and pepper

4 granary rolls or focaccia, split

1. Preheat the grill to medium-high and line the grill pan with foil. Place the turkey, breadcrumbs, onion, apple, lemon rind and juice and parsley in a large bowl. Season to taste with salt and pepper and gently mix to combine. Divide into four equal-sized portions and shape each portion into a patty.

2. Brush the patties with oil and place on the preheated grill pan. Cook under the preheated grill, turning once, for 5 minutes, or until cooked through. Test to check that the juices run clear when the patties are pierced with the point of a knife. If there are any traces of pink, return to the grill for 1–2 minutes.

3. Place a burger on each bun base, add the bun lids and serve immediately.

top tip

Buy minced turkey, keep it
refrigerated and ideally use
within 24 hours of purchase.

cals: 395   fat: 15.2g   sat fat: 3.6g   fibre: 4.1g   carbs: 41.8g   sugar: 7.6g   salt: 2.3g   protein: 23.9g

salmon burgers with pine nuts

prep: 35 mins, plus chilling
cook: 27–36 mins

300 g/10½ oz potatoes,
   peeled and cut into chunks

450 g/1 lb fresh salmon fillet, skinned

175 g/6 oz spinach leaves

55 g/2 oz pine nuts, toasted

2 tbsp finely grated lemon rind

1 tbsp chopped fresh parsley

2 tbsp wholemeal flour

200 ml/7 fl oz crème fraîche

4-cm/1½-inch piece cucumber,
   peeled and finely chopped

2 tbsp sunflower oil

salt and pepper

4–6 wholemeal buns, split

grilled cherry tomatoes, to serve

top tip

Pine nuts add flavour and crunch to these tasty burgers. Toasting them before use enhances their flavour further.

1. This recipe requires a barbecue. Cook the potatoes in a saucepan of lightly salted boiling water for 15–20 minutes, or until tender. Drain well, then mash and reserve. Chop the salmon into chunks.

2. Reserve a few spinach leaves for serving, then blanch the remainder in a saucepan of boiling water for 2 minutes. Drain, squeezing out any excess moisture, then chop.

3. Place the spinach in a food processor or blender with the salmon, potatoes, pine nuts, 1 tablespoon of the lemon rind, the parsley and salt and pepper to taste and, using the pulse button, blend together. Shape into four to six equal-sized burgers, then cover and leave to chill in the refrigerator for 1 hour. Coat the burgers in the flour.

4. Mix the crème fraîche, cucumber and the remaining lemon rind together in a bowl, then cover and leave to chill until required.

5. Preheat the barbecue. Brush the burgers with the oil and cook over medium-hot coals for 4–6 minutes on each side, or until cooked through.

6. Place the reserved spinach leaves on the bottom halves of the buns and top with the burgers, then spoon over a little of the crème fraîche mixture. Add the lids and serve immediately with grilled cherry tomatoes.

serves 6

cals: 583   fat: 35   sat fat: 11.7g   fibre: 6.9g   carbs: 40.3g   sugar: 3.4g   salt: 2g   protein: 26.1g

steakhouse burgers

prep: 25–30 mins, plus chilling
cook: 6–8 mins

450 g/1 lb boneless braising steak or a
mixture with at least 20 per cent fat

1 tsp salt

½ tsp pepper

4 burger buns, split

4 Gruyère cheese slices

2 tbsp mayonnaise

2 tbsp tomato ketchup

lettuce leaves

tomato slices

top tip

For these burgers, choose steak with at least
20 per cent fat, as the fat will add flavour
and helps to baste the meat as it cooks,
keeping the burgers juicy.

1. This recipe requires a barbecue. Preheat
the barbecue to medium-high. Chop the
beef into 2.5-cm/1-inch cubes, then place
on a plate, wrap in clingfilm and chill in the
refrigerator for about 30 minutes.

2. Place half the beef in a food processor
or blender. Pulse (do not run the processor)
about 15 times. Season the meat with half
the salt and half the pepper, and pulse a
further 10–15 times until the meat is finely
chopped but not over-processed. Remove
from the processor and repeat with the
remaining beef. Divide into four equal-sized
portions and shape each portion into a patty.

3. Place the patties on the rack and cook until
brown and cooked to your liking, 3 minutes
on each side for medium rare and 4 minutes
on each side for medium. Place a slice
of cheese on each burger during the last
2 minutes of cooking.

4. Meanwhile, put the mayonnaise and
ketchup into a small bowl and mix to
combine. Spread on the buns, then add the
burgers with the lettuce leaves and tomato
slices. Serve immediately.

serves 4

cals: 626   fat: 38.4g   sat fat: 14.6g   fibre: 1.5g   carbs: 34.5g   sugar: 5.3g   salt: 2.8g   protein: 33.4g

sliders

prep: 20–25 mins
cook: 7–8 mins

450 g/1 lb fresh beef mince

1 tsp salt

½ tsp pepper

1–2 tsp butter

85 g/3 oz Cheddar cheese, sliced and cut into 5-cm/2-inch squares

12 mini burger buns or small bread rolls, split

1. Place the beef in a medium-sized bowl, add the salt and pepper, then divide into 12 equal-sized portions and shape each portion into a patty.

2. Heat a griddle pan over a medium-high heat. Add enough butter to lightly coat the pan, using a spatula to spread it over the base. Add the patties and cook for 3 minutes on one side until brown, then turn and add the cheese. Cook for a further 2–3 minutes, or until brown and cooked to your liking.

3. Place the burgers in the buns and serve immediately.

variation

For a change, try pork or lamb mince and an alternative good melting cheese like Comté or Gruyère.

cals: 156   fat: 7.3g   sat fat: 3.5g   fibre: 1g   carbs: 10.7g   sugar: 1g   salt: 0.9g   protein: 11.3g

how to make the perfect burger patty

Burgers are incredibly easy to prepare, and the only really important step, beyond not overcooking them, is forming the patty. The main thing to avoid is overworking the meat, which can result in tough, rather than tender and juicy, burgers.

Fresh beef mince is the easiest to work with, because it's both dry enough and sticky enough to bind well. Turkey, chicken and pork mince can be much wetter than beef and therefore harder to shape, but adding some breadcrumbs can help with that problem. Also, wetting your hands while forming the patties helps. The same applies to vegetarian burgers, which can be wet and difficult to shape.

To form patties, place the meat in a bowl, add all of the seasonings at once, then mix – preferably with your hands – just until the seasonings are fully integrated.

Divide the meat into portions, then gently form each portion into even-sized patties. If possible, make the patties slightly wider than the buns, because they will shrink during cooking. For the same reason, it also helps to make the edges of the patty thicker than the centre, or to add a dimple to the centre of the patty, so that when the meat contracts, the patty will end up evenly thick.

how to cook the perfect burger

Quick cooking methods with high, dry heat are the best way to get burgers nicely browned on the outside while keeping them juicy inside.

Fried and Griddled

This is the classic diner method, which involves a hot frying pan and some cooking fat. The burgers cook over a medium-high heat until they develop a golden brown crust.

Steamed

Steaming takes frying one step further to keep the meat extra-moist. While frying, just cover the burgers with a lid to finish cooking.

Barbecued

Charcoal barbecues provide a smoky flavour. To check the heat level of your barbecue hold your hand about 2.5 cm/1 inch above the cooking grate.

The time it takes to get uncomfortably hot determines how hot the grill is:
high: about 3 seconds
medium-high: about 5 seconds
medium: about 7 seconds

Smoked

A foil pouch of wood chips creates smoke that infuses its flavour into burgers cooking in a covered barbecue. Different kinds of wood create different flavours. Smoking on a barbecue requires a barbecue with a lid or hood.

Grilled

A low-mess method that works especially well for fish, poultry or vegetarian burgers, which tend to stick to the rack. It is also a great alternative for any recipe that calls for grilling when the weather doesn't say 'outdoor cooking'.

jamaican jerk chicken burgers

cook: 17 mins, plus standing

1 tsp soft light brown sugar

1 tsp ground ginger

½ tsp ground allspice

½ tsp dried thyme

½–1 tsp cayenne pepper or chopped fresh jalapeño chilli

1 tbsp lime juice

2 garlic cloves, finely chopped

½ tsp salt

½ tsp pepper

450 g/1 lb fresh chicken mince

1 tbsp vegetable oil

1 red pepper or yellow pepper, deseeded and cut into large flat pieces

1 tsp olive oil

1 tsp red wine vinegar

4 onion rolls, split

lettuce leaves

salt and pepper

top tip

Swap turkey or pork mince for the chicken mince. Roast sweet potato wedges provide the perfect accompaniment to these tasty burgers.

1. Place the sugar, ginger, allspice, thyme, cayenne pepper, lime juice, garlic, the salt and pepper into a bowl and mix together. Add the chicken and gently mix to combine. Divide the mixture into four equal-sized portions and shape each portion into a patty.

2. Place a griddle pan over a medium-high heat and add the vegetable oil. Add the red pepper and cook for about 5 minutes, turning frequently, until blackened. Transfer to a bowl, cover with clingfilm or a plate and leave to steam for 5 minutes. Remove the skin and cut the flesh into strips. Toss with the olive oil, vinegar, and salt and pepper to taste.

3. Put the patties in the pan and cook, covered, for about 5 minutes on each side until brown and cooked through. Place the burgers in the rolls and top with the lettuce and peppers. Serve immediately.

cals: 446   fat: 17.4g   sat fat: 4.1g   fibre: 3.3g   carbs: 46.4g   sugar: 7.7g   salt: 1.9g   protein: 26.4g

barbecued cajun pork burgers

prep: 20 mins, plus chilling
cook: 35-45 mins

225 g/8 oz sweet potatoes,
  cut into chunks

450 g/1 lb fresh pork mince

1 eating apple, peeled, cored and
  grated

2 tsp Cajun seasoning

450 g/1 lb onions

1 tbsp chopped fresh coriander

2 tbsp sunflower oil

8–12 lean back bacon rashers

salt and pepper

top tip

To keep coriander fresh for longer store
it in the salad drawer of the refrigerator
wrapped in damp kitchen paper.

1. This recipe requires a barbecue. Cook the sweet potato in a saucepan of lightly salted boiling water for 15–20 minutes, or until soft when pierced with a fork. Drain well, then mash and reserve.

2. Place the pork in a bowl, add the mashed potato, apple and Cajun seasoning. Grate one of the onions and add to the pork mixture with the coriander and salt and pepper to taste. Mix together, then shape into four to six equal-sized patties. Cover and leave to chill in the refrigerator for 1 hour.

3. Slice the remaining onions. Heat 1 tablespoon of the oil in a frying pan. Add the onions and cook over a low heat for 10–12 minutes, stirring until soft. Remove the frying pan from the heat and reserve. Wrap each patty in two bacon rashers.

4. Preheat the barbecue. Cook the patties over hot coals, brushing with the remaining oil, for 4–5 minutes on each side, or until thoroughly cooked. Alternatively, cook in a ridged griddle pan or under a hot grill. Serve immediately with the fried onions.

serves 6

cals: 375   fat: 22.9g   sat fat: 7.4g   fibre: 5.8g   carbs: 18g   sugar: 7g   salt: 2.4g   protein: 28.3g

blue cheese-stuffed burgers

prep: 20 mins
cook: 10–12 mins

550 g/1 lb 4 oz fresh beef mince

1 tsp salt

½ tsp pepper

55–85 g/2–3 oz blue cheese,
    cut into 4 chunks

vegetable oil, for frying

4 brioche buns, split

lettuce leaves

tomato slices

red onion slices

1. Place the mince in a medium-sized bowl with the salt and pepper and gently mix to combine. Divide into four equal-sized portions and roll each portion into a ball. Use your finger to make a hole in each ball, then stuff a chunk of cheese inside. Press to seal the outside and flatten into 1-cm/½-inch thick patties.

2. Place a large, non-stick frying pan or ridged griddle pan over a medium-high heat. Add enough vegetable oil to just cover the base, then add the patties and cook for 4–5 minutes on each side until brown and cooked through (some cheese may escape).

3. Put the burgers in the buns, top with the lettuce leaves, tomato and onion and serve immediately.

top tip

Blue cheese such as Stilton,
dolcelatte or Gorgonzola, adds a
wonderful flavour to these
delicious burgers.

cals: 577   fat: 29.2g   sat fat: 13.2g   fibre: 1.4g   carbs: 39.3g   sugar: 7.5g   salt: 3.2g   protein: 36.8g

smoky trout burgers with pesto relish

prep: 30 mins, plus chilling
cook: 23-30 mins

225 g/8 oz potatoes, cut into chunks

salt and pepper

350 g/12 oz smoked trout fillets, flaked

2 tsp creamed horseradish

6 spring onions, finely chopped

175 g/6 oz courgette, roughly grated

2 tbsp wholemeal flour

8 lean back bacon rashers

2 tbsp sunflower oil

pesto relish

15 g/½ oz fresh basil

40 g/1½ oz pine nuts, toasted

3 garlic cloves

150 ml/5 fl oz virgin olive oil

40 g/1½ oz Parmesan cheese, freshly grated

4-cm/1½-inch piece cucumber, peeled and finely diced

4 spring onions, finely chopped

2 plum tomatoes, finely diced

top tip

Basil is a tender herb with an aromatic flavour and it is an essential ingredient in pesto. It has an affinity with tomatoes and adds delicious flavour to this relish.

1. This recipe requires a barbecue. Cook the potatoes in a saucepan of lightly salted water for 15–20 minutes, or until cooked. Drain, mash and place in a large bowl.

Add the trout, horseradish, spring onions, courgette and salt and pepper to taste. Mix together and shape into four equal-sized burgers. Leave to chill for 1 hour, then coat in the flour and wrap each in two rashers of bacon. Preheat the barbecue.

2. Meanwhile, prepare the relish. Place the basil, pine nuts and garlic in a food processor and blend for 1 minute. With the motor running, gradually pour in the oil and continue to blend until all the oil has been incorporated. Scrape into a bowl and stir in the cheese, cucumber, spring onions and tomatoes. Spoon into a serving bowl.

3. Lightly brush the burgers with oil and then cook over medium-hot coals for 3-4 minutes on each side until golden and piping hot. Serve.

cals: 790   fat: 54.7g   sat fat: 10.4g   fibre: 4.8g   carbs: 26g   sugar: 4.5g   salt: 4.3g   protein: 41g

green chilli cheeseburgers

prep: 25 mins
cook: 15 mins, plus standing

3 large mild green chillies

675 g/1 lb 8 oz fresh lean beef mince

1 tsp salt

115 g/4 oz Cheddar cheese, grated, plus 6 thin slices

6 soft burger buns, split

1. This recipe requires a barbecue. Preheat the barbecue to high. Place the chillies on the rack and cook, turning frequently, until black all over. Wrap them in foil and leave to stand for 15 minutes. Peel off the skins, remove the stems and finely chop.

2. Put the mince, salt, chopped chillies and grated cheese into a large bowl and gently mix to combine.

3. Divide the mixture into six equal-sized portions and form each portion into a patty. Place the patties on the rack and cook for 4 minutes. Turn, top each burger with a slice of cheese, then cover and cook for a further 4 minutes until cooked to your liking and the cheese is melted. Place the burgers in the buns and serve immediately.

top tip

Crisp French fries and a mixed baby leaf salad are ideal accompaniments for these simple barbecued burgers.

cals: 525   fat: 25.9g   sat fat: 13g   fibre: 1.2g   carbs: 33.5g   sugar: 3.7g   salt: 2.4g   protein: 37.9g

london burgers

prep: 20 mins
cook: 15 mins

450 g/1 lb fresh beef mince
2 tbsp Worcestershire sauce
4 muffins
4 tbsp butter
2 tsp vegetable oil
4 eggs
½ tsp salt
½ tsp pepper

1. Combine the mince with half the Worcestershire sauce in a large bowl. Divide the mixture into four equal-sized portions and shape each portion into a patty about 1 cm/½ inch wider than the muffins, making a dimple in the centre of each patty.

2. Split the muffins and spread each half with butter.

3. Heat a large frying pan over a medium-high heat. Place the muffin halves in the pan buttered side down and cook for about 2 minutes.

4. Add the patties to the pan and cook for about 4 minutes until brown. Turn and cook on the other side for 4 minutes, or until cooked to your liking. Place a burger on one of the muffin halves on each plate and drizzle with the remaining Worcestershire sauce.

5. Add the oil to the pan, swirling to coat. Add the eggs and sprinkle with the salt and pepper. Cover and cook for about 3 minutes until the whites are set and the yolks are beginning to set at the edges. Top each burger with an egg and the top half of a muffin. Serve immediately.

variation

Try poached eggs instead of fried, and swap soft rolls for the muffins.

cals: 610   fat: 36g   sat fat: 14.7g   fibre: 2g   carbs: 32.5g   sugar: 4.9g   salt: 2.4g   protein: 35.8g

pork burgers with tangy orange marinade

prep: 25 mins, plus marinating and chilling
cook: 30-40 mins

450 g/1 lb pork fillet, cut into
   small pieces

3 tbsp Seville orange marmalade

2 tbsp orange juice

1 tbsp balsamic vinegar

225 g/8 oz parsnips,
   cut into chunks

1 tbsp finely grated orange rind

2 garlic cloves, crushed

6 spring onions, finely chopped

1 courgette (175 g/6 oz), grated

salt and pepper

1 tbsp sunflower oil

top tip

Serve these tasty burgers in seed-topped burger buns with the marinade spooned on top and with a few salad leaves tucked in.

1. This recipe requires a barbecue. Place the pork in a shallow dish. Place the marmalade, orange juice and vinegar in a small saucepan and heat, stirring, until the marmalade has melted. Pour the marinade over the pork. Cover and leave for at least 30 minutes, or longer if time permits. Remove the pork, reserving the marinade. Mince the pork into a large bowl.

2. Meanwhile, cook the parsnips in a saucepan of boiling water for 15–20 minutes, or until cooked. Drain, then mash and add to the pork. Stir in the orange rind, garlic, spring onions, courgette and salt and pepper to taste. Mix together, then shape into six patties. Cover and leave to chill for at least 30 minutes.

3. Preheat the barbecue. Lightly brush each burger with a little oil and then add them to the barbecue grill, cooking over medium-hot coals for 4-6 minutes on each side or until thoroughly cooked. Boil the reserved marinade for 3 minutes, then pour into a small jug or bowl. Serve.

serves 6

cals: 159   fat: 4.1g   sat fat: 0.8g   fibre: 2.8g   carbs: 13.9g   sugar: 7.3g   salt: 1.4g   protein: 16.7g

The definition of a side doesn't have to be, 'a soggy piece of lettuce and half a tomato.' There is a vast array of fun and flavoursome side orders to get excited about and they should be easy to create and magnificent to munch. Whether part of a main or a sneaky snack, get on board with a side.

a bit on the side

coleslaw

prep: 20 mins, plus chilling
cook: no cooking

150 ml/5 fl oz mayonnaise
150 ml/5 fl oz natural yogurt
dash of Tabasco sauce
1 head of white cabbage
4 carrots
1 green pepper
salt and pepper

1. To make the dressing, mix the mayonnaise, yogurt, Tabasco sauce and salt and pepper to taste together in a small bowl. Chill in the refrigerator until required.

2. Cut the cabbage in half and then into quarters. Remove and discard the tough centre stalk. Finely shred the cabbage leaves. Wash the leaves under cold running water and dry thoroughly on kitchen paper. Peel the carrots and roughly grate or shred in a food processor or on a mandoline. Quarter and deseed the pepper and cut the flesh into thin strips.

3. Mix the vegetables together in a large serving bowl and toss to mix. Pour over the dressing and toss until the vegetables are well coated. Cover and chill in the refrigerator until required.

variation

Try nuts, seeds, apple, raisins and capers. Cheese also adds a great twist

sweetcorn relish (sweetcorn chow chow)

prep: 20-25 mins, plus cooling
cook: 20 mins

3 corn cobs
1 red pepper
1 jalapeño chilli
125 ml/4 fl oz cider vinegar
100 g/3½ oz soft light brown sugar
1 tbsp salt
1 tbsp ground mustard seeds
½ tsp celery seeds
1 red onion, diced

1. Cut the kernels off the corn cobs. Deseed and dice the red pepper and the chilli.

2. Put the corn, red pepper, chilli, vinegar, sugar, salt, mustard seeds and celery seeds into a large saucepan over a medium-high heat and bring to the boil. Reduce the heat to simmering and cook, stirring occasionally, for about 15 minutes until the mixture reduces slightly. The sugar will melt, producing enough liquid to cover the vegetables.

3. Stir the onions into the corn mixture, remove from the heat and ladle the relish into sterilized jars. Seal with lids and leave to cool to room temperature.

top tip

This tasty relish, laced with mustard seeds, will keep for up to 1 month in the refrigerator.

makes 950 g

cals: 799   fat: 7g   sat fat: 0.2g   fibre: 12g   carbs: 181g   sugar: 131.7g   salt: 19.5g   protein: 14.6g

barbecue sauce

prep: 20 mins, plus optional cooling
cook: 25 mins

1 tbsp olive oil

1 small onion, finely chopped

2–3 garlic cloves, crushed

1 red jalapeño chilli, deseeded and
finely chopped (optional)

2 tsp tomato purée

1 tsp (or to taste) dry mustard

1 tbsp red wine vinegar

1 tbsp Worcestershire sauce

2–3 tsp muscovado sugar

300 ml/10 fl oz water

1. Heat the oil in a small heavy-based saucepan, add the onion, garlic and chilli, if using, and gently sauté, stirring frequently, for 3 minutes, or until beginning to soften. Remove from the heat.

2. Blend the tomato purée with the mustard, the vinegar and the Worcestershire sauce to a paste, then stir into the onion mixture with 2 teaspoons of the sugar. Mix well, then gradually stir in the water.

3. Return to the heat and bring to the boil, stirring frequently. Reduce the heat and gently simmer, stirring occasionally, for 15 minutes. Taste and add the remaining sugar, if liked. Strain, if preferred, and serve hot or leave to cool and serve cold.

makes 225 ml

top tip

Barbecue sauce is the ultimate
burger accompaniment; it makes
the average burger extra special.

cals: 289   fat: 11.4g   sat fat: 1.8g   fibre: 3.3g   carbs: 37.9g   sugar: 25.8g   salt: 0.6g   protein: 3.6g

fiery roasted tomato sauce

prep: 25 mins, plus cooling
cook: 45 mins

6 vine-ripened tomatoes

1 red pepper, cut into quarters and deseeded

1 garlic clove, unpeeled

1 red onion, cut into quarters

4 tbsp olive oil

1 small red jalapeño chilli, very finely chopped

1 tsp hot paprika

1 tbsp sherry

salt and pepper

top tip

This scrumptious chilli-spiced sauce is great for dipping or as an accompaniment to chargrilled burgers, sausages and chicken legs or thighs.

1. Preheat the oven to 180°C/350°F/Gas Mark 4.

2. Lay out the vegetables on a large baking tray, brush with olive oil, then roast in the oven, turning once halfway through cooking, for about 45 minutes or until they are blistered and slightly charred.

3. Leave to cool. When cool enough to handle, peel the tomatoes and red pepper, and squeeze the garlic from its skin. Transfer the tomato, red pepper, garlic flesh and onion to a food processor and process to a fairly smooth consistency.

4. Spoon the mixture into a large serving bowl and stir in the chilli, paprika and sherry. Season to taste. The sauce can be used immediately or left to cool completely and stored in an airtight container in the refrigerator for up to 1 week.

makes 175 ml

cals: 730   fat: 56.1g   sat fat: 7.4g   fibre: 14.2g   carbs: 50.8g   sugar: 29.1g   salt: 6g   protein: 9.3g

smoky bbq beans

prep: 15 mins
cook: 32 mins

4 tbsp olive oil

1 large onion, chopped

2 garlic cloves, chopped

2 celery sticks, chopped

1 large carrot, chopped

1 tsp fennel seeds

2 tsp dried oregano

2 tsp smoked paprika

1 tbsp chipotle paste

1 tbsp molasses

450 ml/16 fl oz passata

400 g/14 oz canned cannellini beans, drained

salt and pepper, to taste

1. Heat the oil in a large saucepan over a medium heat. Add the onion, garlic, celery and carrot and sweat with a lid on for 15 minutes, or until translucent and softened.

2. Add the fennel seeds, oregano, paprika, chipotle and molasses. Cook for 5 minutes to allow the sugars to start to caramelize.

3. Add the passata and beans and cook for a further 10 minutes.

4. Season with salt and pepper and serve.

serves 4

top tip

For the meat loving carnivore try adding smoked bacon or chorizo.

cals: 270   fat: 14.3g   sat fat: 2g   fibre: 7.9g   carbs: 29g   sugar: 13g   salt: 2.1g   protein: 7g

chipotle ketchup & chipotle mustard

prep: 15 mins, plus cooling and chilling
cook: 8–10 mins

chipotle ketchup

225 ml/8 fl oz prepared tomato ketchup

½ tsp Worcestershire sauce

½ tsp light brown sugar

1 tbsp fresh lemon juice, or to taste

1½ tsp chipotle powder, or to taste

1 tsp ground cumin

½ tsp ground turmeric

¼ tsp ground ginger

salt

chipotle mustard

125 ml/4 fl oz Dijon mustard

1 tsp chipotle powder, or to taste

top tip

Chipotle is a dried, smoked jalapeño — it is used frequently in Mexican cooking and adds a great, distinctive smoky flavour to any dish.

1. For the ketchup, combine all the ingredients with salt to taste in a small saucepan and place over a medium heat. Bring to a simmer and cook, stirring frequently, for 5 minutes, or until the ketchup is slightly thickened. Remove from the heat and cool. Transfer to a sterilized jar, cover, and refrigerate until ready to use.

2. To make the chipotle mustard, place the ingredients in a small bowl and stir to thoroughly combine. Transfer to a sterilized jar, cover, and refrigerate until ready to use.

makes 225 ml

makes 125 ml

cals: 273   fat: 0.8g   sat fat: trace   fibre: 3.6g   carbs: 62.2g   sugar: 56.7g   salt: 8g   protein: 3.5g

garlic bread

prep: 15 mins
cook: 10–15 mins

150 g/5½ oz butter, softened
3 cloves garlic, crushed
2 tbsp chopped fresh flat-leaf parsley
pepper
1 large or 2 small sticks of
   French bread

1. This recipe requires a barbecue. Preheat the barbecue. Mix the butter, garlic and parsley together in a bowl until well combined. Season to taste with pepper and mix well.

2. Make several lengthways cuts in the bread but be careful not to cut all the way through.

3. Spread the flavoured butter over one side of each cut and place the loaf on a large sheet of double-thickness aluminium foil.

4. Wrap the bread in the aluminium foil and cook over hot coals for 10–15 minutes, until the butter melts and the bread is piping hot. Serve immediately.

top tip

When buying garlic, choose firm bulbs with tightly packed cloves and unwrinkled skin. Soft, shrivelled or sprouting garlic should be avoided.

serves 6

cals: 376   fat: 21.6g   sat fat: 13.2g   fibre: 1.8g   carbs: 38.5g   sugar: 1.7g   salt: 1.3g   protein: 9.1g

caramelized onions

prep: 10 mins
cook: 25 mins

1–2 tbsp vegetable oil or olive oil

½ red onion, sliced

½ tsp finely chopped fresh rosemary, thyme or oregano (optional)

½ tsp red wine vinegar

salt and pepper

top tip

Caramelized onions are both rich and sweet. They are easy to cook, making them the perfect burger topping.

1. Heat enough oil to coat the base of a large frying pan over a medium heat until shimmering. Add the onion and cook on one side for 3 minutes until brown. Add the herbs, if using, stir and continue cooking, stirring occasionally, for about 12 minutes until nicely browned.

2. Season to taste with salt and pepper. Add the vinegar and cook for a further 8–10 minutes until very soft.

3. Serve immediately or leave to cool and store in the refrigerator for up to 3 days.

cals: 61   fat: 5.1g   sat fat: 0.5g   fibre: 0.7g   carbs: 3.7g   sugar: 1.6g   salt: 1.5g   protein: 0.4g

rubs and marinades

Marinades and rubs are a great way of adding flavour to all types of food and are speedy and simple to prepare, they need only to be left for a while to work their magic in advance of cooking.

chilli espresso rub

makes about 5 tbsp

creole rub

makes about 10 tbsp

2 tbsp pepper
2 tbsp celery salt
2 tbsp paprika
4 tsp garlic powder

4 tsp dried thyme
2 tsp dried oregano
2 tsp ground bay leaves
pinch of chilli powder

2 tbsp dark brown sugar
1 tbsp ground espresso coffee
1 tbsp ground coriander
2 tsp ground cumin
1 tsp ground ginger
1–2 tsp dried red chilli flakes or chilli powder
salt and pepper

1. Mix all the ingredients together in a small bowl until thoroughly combined.

2. Rub the mixture thoroughly into meat, poultry, fish or seafood 1–2 hours before cooking.

3. Put in a shallow dish, cover tightly and chill in the refrigerator until required.

1. Mix all the ingredients together in a small bowl until thoroughly combined.

2. Rub the mixture thoroughly into the meat, poultry, fish or seafood up to 6 hours before cooking.

3. Put in shallow dish, cover tightly and chill in the refrigerator until required.

spicy beer marinade

makes enough for about 500 g/1 lb 2 oz meat or game

350 ml/12 fl oz beer
5 tbsp soy sauce
1 tbsp Worcestershire sauce
1 tsp Tabasco sauce
1 garlic clove, finely chopped
1 tbsp wholegrain mustard
2 tsp paprika
1 tsp salt
1 tsp pepper

1. Score the meat or game portions deeply with a sharp knife. Put the prepared meat or game in a shallow non-metallic dish or place in a food bag.

2. Whisk all the ingredients together in a small bowl until thoroughly combined.

3. Pour the marinade over the prepared meat or game and turn to coat.

4. Cover tightly or seal and let marinate in the refrigerator, turning occasionally, for up to 6 hours before cooking.

spanish-style marinade

makes enough for about 500 g/1 lb 2 oz meat, poultry, fish or seafood.

150 g/5½ oz soft light brown sugar
5 tbsp orange marmalade
2 tbsp freshly squeezed Seville orange juice
2 tbsp tomato purée
1 tbsp wholegrain mustard

1. Score the meat, poultry or fish portions deeply with a sharp knife. Put the prepared meat, poultry, fish or seafood in a shallow non-metallic dish or plastic food bag.

2. Heat all the ingredients in a pan over low heat, stirring until smooth. Remove from the heat and let cool.

3. Pour the marinade over the prepared meat, poultry, fish or seafood and turn to coat.

4. Cover tightly or seal and let marinate in the refrigerator, turning occasionally, for up to 12 hours before cooking.

quick pickled onions

prep: 15 mins
cook: no cooking

225 ml/8 fl oz distilled white vinegar
100 g/3½ oz sugar
1 tsp chipotle powder, or to taste
2 medium red onions, cut into rings
salt

top tip

The onion is a top health food, containing sulphur compounds that are natural antibiotics to help protect from cancers and heart disease.

1. In a medium bowl, combine the vinegar, sugar, chipotle powder, and salt to taste. Whisk to dissolve the sugar.

2. Place the onions in a heavy-duty, zip-top bag and pour the marinade over the onions. Toss to coat. Cover and refrigerate for 30 minutes, moving the mixture around a couple of times to evenly distribute the marinade. Drain before serving.

makes 450 g

cals: 558   fat: 0.2g   sat fat: trace   fibre: 6g   carbs: 129.4g   sugar: 112.8g   salt: 6g   protein: 3.9g

guacamole

prep: 15-20 mins
cook: no cooking

2 large ripe avocados
juice of 1 lime, or to taste
2 tsp olive oil
½ onion, finely chopped
1 green chilli, such as poblano, deseeded and finely chopped
1 garlic clove, crushed
¼ tsp ground cumin
1 tbsp chopped fresh coriander, plus extra sprigs to garnish
salt and pepper

top tip

To ripen an avocado, put it in a brown paper bag with a banana at room temperature. Bananas release ethylene, which speeds up the ripening process.

1. Cut the avocados in half lengthways and twist the halves in opposite directions to separate. Stab the stone with the point of a sharp knife and lift out. Peel, then roughly chop the avocado halves and place in a non-metallic bowl. Squeeze over the lime juice and add the oil.

2. Mash the avocados with a fork to the desired consistency – either chunky or smooth. Mix in the onion, chilli, garlic, cumin and chopped coriander, then season to taste with salt and pepper.

3. Transfer to a serving dish and serve immediately to avoid discoloration, garnished with coriander sprigs.

cals: 218   fat: 18.3g   sat fat: 2.7g   fibre: 9.1g   carbs: 15.1g   sugar: 2.4g   salt: 1.5g   protein: 3.1g

ranch dressing

175 ml/6 fl oz buttermilk

175 ml/6 fl oz soured cream

2 tbsp finely chopped fresh flat-leaf parsley

2 tbsp finely chopped spring onions

2 tbsp finely chopped celery

2 tsp finely chopped fresh dill

1 tbsp lemon juice

1 garlic clove, finely chopped

½ tsp mustard powder

½ tsp salt

½ tsp pepper

1. Put the buttermilk and soured cream into a bowl and mix together until well combined. Add the remaining ingredients and stir to mix well.

2. To store, cover and refrigerate for up to 1 week.

top tip

Packed with fresh herbs, creamy ranch dressing is a surprisingly refreshing dip for your favourite style of chips.

makes 450 ml

cals: 117   fat: 7.6g   sat fat: 5.5g   fibre: 0.5g   carbs: 5.2g   sugar: 4.2g   salt: 0.9g   protein: 3.1g

chips

prep: 25 mins, plus soaking and cooling
cook: 35-40 mins

675 g/1 lb 8 oz large potatoes
sunflower, corn or groundnut oil,
   for deep-frying
salt and pepper

top tip

Call them what you wish, but any burger
from the most simple to gourmet,
wouldn't be the same without this
classic accompaniment

1. Peel the potatoes and cut into 8-mm/
⅜-inch even-sized fingers. As soon as they
are prepared, put them into a large bowl
of cold water to prevent discoloration,
then leave them to soak for 30 minutes
to remove the excess starch.

2. Drain the potatoes and dry well on a
clean tea towel. Heat the oil in a deep-
fat fryer or large, heavy-based saucepan
to 190°C/375°F. If you do not have a
thermometer, test the temperature by
dropping a potato finger into the oil. If it
sinks, the oil isn't hot enough; if it floats and
the oil bubbles around the potato, it is ready.

3. Carefully add a small batch of potatoes to
the oil (this is to ensure even cooking and to
avoid reducing the temperature of the oil) and
deep-fry for 5–6 minutes until soft but not
browned. Remove from the oil and drain well
on kitchen paper. Leave to cool for at least 5
minutes. Continue to deep-fry the remaining
potatoes in the same way, allowing the oil to
return to the correct temperature each time.

4. When ready to serve, reheat the oil to
200°C/400°F. Add the potatoes, in small
batches and deep-fry for 2–3 minutes until
golden brown. Remove from the oil and drain
on kitchen paper. Serve immediately, seasoned
to taste with salt and pepper.

serves 4

cals: 258   fat: 18g   sat fat: 1.8g   fibre: 1.9g   carbs: 23.8g   sugar: 0.8g   salt: 1.5g   protein: 2.9g

crispy onion rings

115 g/4 oz plain flour
pinch of salt
1 egg
150 ml/5 fl oz semi-skimmed milk
4 large onions
vegetable oil, for deep-frying
chilli powder, to taste (optional)
salt and pepper
lettuce leaves, to serve (optional)

top tip

There are dozens of methods that claim to prevent crying while cutting onions, from peeling them under running water to whistling while you work!

1. To make the batter, sift the flour and a pinch of salt into a large bowl and make a well in the centre. Break the egg into the well and gently beat with a whisk. Gradually whisk in the milk, drawing the flour from the side into the liquid in the centre to form a smooth batter.

2. Leaving the onions whole, slice widthways into 5-mm/¼-inch slices, then separate each slice into rings.

3. Heat the oil in a deep-fat fryer or deep, heavy-based saucepan to 180–190°C/350–375°F, or until a cube of bread browns in 30 seconds.

4. Using the tines of a fork, pick up several onions rings at a time and dip in the batter. Let any excess batter drip off, then add the onions to the oil and deep-fry for 1–2 minutes until they rise to the surface of the oil and become crisp and golden brown. Remove from the oil, drain on kitchen paper and keep warm while deep-frying the remaining onion rings in batches. Do not try to deep-fry too many at a time, as this will reduce the temperature of the oil and the onion rings will absorb some of the oil and become soggy.

5. Season the onion rings with chilli powder, if wished, and salt and pepper to taste, then serve immediately on a bed of lettuce leaves.

serves 6

cals: 294   fat: 18.3g   sat fat: 2.3g   fibre: 2.7g   carbs: 28g   sugar: 6.7g   salt: 1.4g   protein: 5.4g

sweet potato chips

vegetable oil for deep frying

60 g/2¼ oz plain flour, plus extra
   if needed

1 tsp salt

225 ml/8 fl oz water, plus extra
   if needed

900 g/2 lb orange-fleshed sweet
   potatoes, peeled and cut into
   5-mm/¼-inch sticks

salt

1. Place the oil in a large, heavy-based saucepan or a deep-fryer. If using a saucepan, attach a deep-frying thermometer. Heat the oil to 180–190°C/350–375°F, or until a cube of bread browns in 30 seconds.

2. Meanwhile, combine the flour and salt in a medium-sized bowl. Whisk in the water until well combined. The batter should be the consistency of a very thin pancake batter. If it is too thick, add more water, 1 tablespoon at a time. If it is too thin, add more flour, 1 tablespoon at a time.

3. Add a handful of the sweet potatoes to the batter and stir to coat. Remove from the batter using tongs, allowing the excess to drip back into the bowl. Transfer the battered potatoes to the hot oil and cook for 3–4 minutes, until golden brown and crisp. Remove using tongs and drain on a plate lined with kitchen paper. Continue cooking in batches until all of the potatoes are cooked. Season generously with salt and serve immediately.

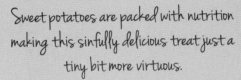

top tip

Sweet potatoes are packed with nutrition making this sinfully delicious treat just a tiny bit more virtuous.

cals: 423   fat: 22.7g   sat fat: 3g   fibre: 6.4g   carbs: 51.2g   sugar: 8.4g   salt: 4.8g   protein: 4.6g

spicy salsa

prep: 15-20 mins
cook: 15-20 mins

vegetable oil spray

8 plum tomatoes, halved

2–4 jalapeño chillies, to taste, halved, cored and deseeded

4 garlic cloves

1 large onion, cut into wedges

25 g/1 oz fresh coriander

4 tbsp lime juice

salt

1. Preheat the oven to 230°C/450°F/Gas Mark 8 and spray a baking sheet with oil.

2. Place the tomatoes, jalapeños, garlic and onion on the prepared baking sheet and lightly spray with oil. Sprinkle with a little salt and roast in the preheated oven for about 15–20 minutes, until the vegetables soften and begin to brown.

3. Place the vegetables in a food processor and pulse to a chunky purée. Add the coriander, lime juice and 1 teaspoon of salt and pulse until the coriander is chopped and all of the ingredients are well combined.

4. To store, cover and refrigerate for up to 1 week.

serves 4

cals: 70   fat: 1g   sat fat: trace   fibre: 3.2g   carbs: 14.7g   sugar: 7.4g   salt: 1.5g   protein: 2.6g

creamy potato salad

prep: 20–25 mins
cook: 25–35 mins

1.25 kg/2 lb 12 oz waxy potatoes

125 ml/4 fl oz mayonnaise

50 ml/2 fl oz soured cream

90 ml/3 fl oz white wine vinegar

1 tsp wholegrain mustard

½ tsp dried dill

75 g/2¾ oz red onions, finely chopped

30 g/1 oz celery, finely chopped

2 tbsp chopped gherkins

40 g/1½ oz roasted red peppers, chopped

2 hard-boiled eggs, chopped (optional)

salt and pepper

top tip

There are many variations of this recipe from all over the world. They vary widely in ingredients and even in the temperature at which the dish is served.

1. Place the unpeeled potatoes in a medium-sized saucepan and cover with water by a few inches. Add salt, bring to the boil over a high heat, then reduce the heat and simmer for 20–30 minutes until tender.

2. Put the mayonnaise, soured cream, vinegar, mustard, dill, and salt and pepper to taste into a bowl and mix together.

3. Drain the potatoes and leave to cool slightly, then slip off the skins with your fingers or with a paring knife. Chop the potatoes into 1-cm/½-inch pieces and add to the dressing while still warm. Stir in the onion, celery, gherkins, peppers and egg, if using. Cover and chill for at least 2 hours or overnight.

serves 8

cals: 274g   fat: 15.1g   sat fat: 2.2g   fibre: 3.2g   carbs: 29.8g   sugar: 2.6g   salt: 2.1g   protein: 4.7g

macaroni salad

prep: 15-20 mins, plus cooling & chilling
cook: 12-15 mins

225 g/8 oz dried elbow macaroni

50 ml/2 fl oz mayonnaise, plus extra if needed

50 ml/2 fl oz natural yogurt

1 tbsp fresh lemon juice

½ tsp garlic salt

½ tsp pepper

40 g/1½ oz celery, diced

40 g/1½ oz spring onions, finely chopped

40 g/1½ oz black olives, finely chopped

50 g/1¾ oz tomatoes, finely chopped

2 tbsp chopped fresh flat-leaf parsley

salt and pepper

top tip

One of the most popular add-ons to this American BBQ staple is hard-boiled eggs. Simply hard-boil three eggs and chop before adding to the bowl with the rest of the ingredients.

1. Bring a medium-sized saucepan of lightly salted water to the boil, add the macaroni and cook according to the packet instructions. Drain.

2. Meanwhile, combine the mayonnaise, yogurt, lemon juice, garlic salt and the pepper in a large bowl. Stir in the hot macaroni, then add the celery, spring onions, olives, tomatoes and parsley. Season to taste with salt and pepper and add more mayonnaise if it seems dry, then leave to cool completely.

3. Cover with clingfilm and chill for at least 2 hours until cold. Serve cold. The salad will keep in the refrigerator for up to 3 days.

serves 6–8

cals: 218   fat: 7.9g   sat fat: 0.8   fibre: 1.9g   carbs: 30.6g   sugar: 2.2g   salt: 1.6g   protein: 5.8g

index